Nostalgic NORTHAMPTON

The publishers would like to thank the following companies for their support in the production of this book

Main sponsor

Sight and Sound Technology

A Bell & Company

C. Butt Ltd

Cosworth

Dickens Brothers Ltd

E. Gallone Ltd

The Grosvenor Shopping Centre

Michael Jones Jewellers

Moulton College

Richard Finch & Sons

Sheinman Opticians

Springline Ltd

Stantone Mechanical Handling

T & K Precision

Wardle & Keach International Ltd

Westbridge Motors

Weston Favell Shopping Centre

First published in Great Britain by True North Books Limited
England HX3 6SN
01422 244555
www.truenorthbooks.com

ISBN 978 - 1906649739

Text, design and origination by True North Books
Printed and bound by The Amadeus Press

Nostalgic NORTHAMPTON

CONTENTS

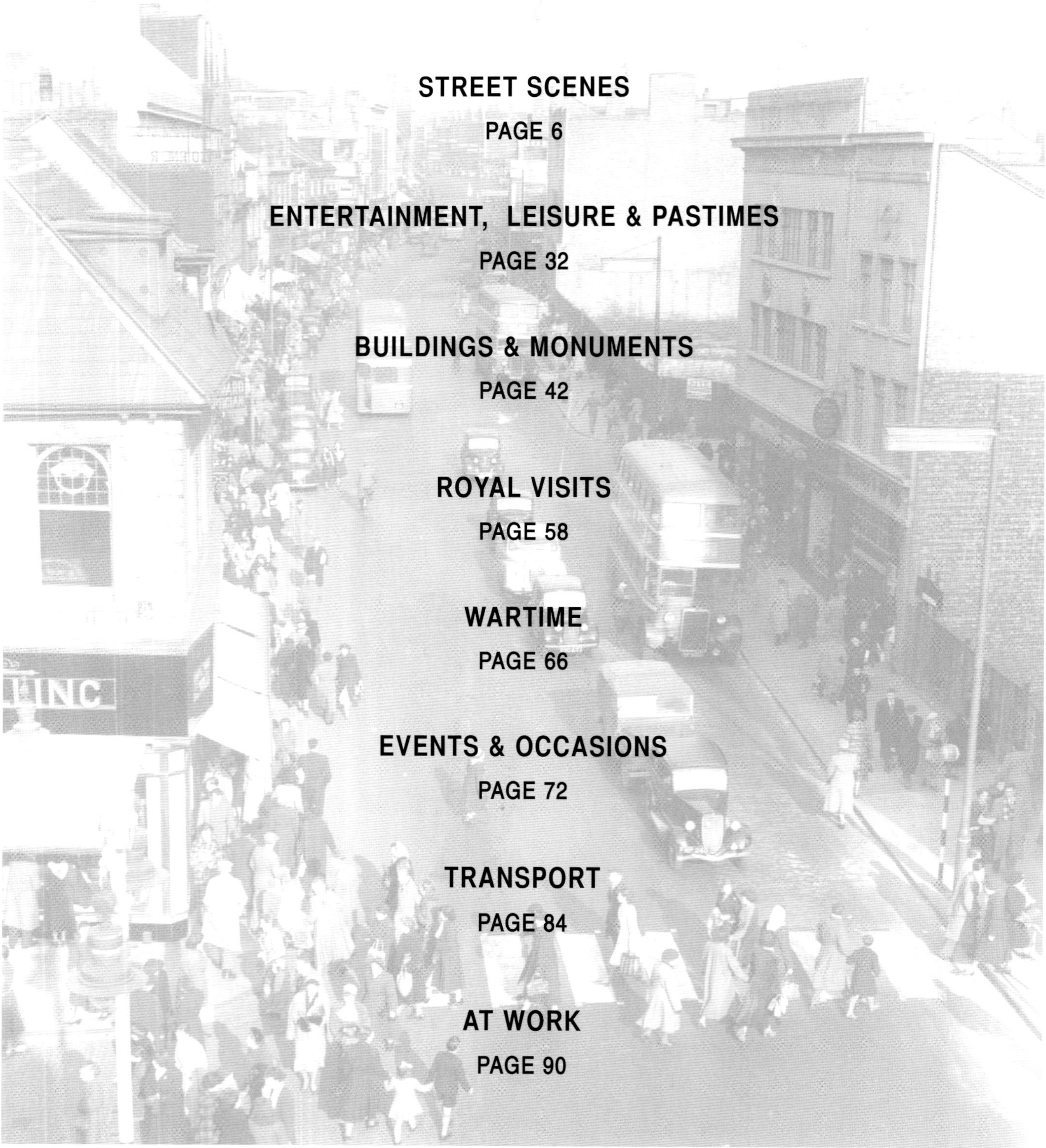

INTRODUCTION

We have returned to this fine town to produce another in the True North series of books on the pride of the East Midlands. 'Nostalgic Northampton' contains a whole raft of images from the last century. Accompanied by informative and interesting text, they take readers back to times that older ones have half forgotten and younger ones have only heard of from their parents and grandparents. This is a place steeped in tradition, dating back to settlements in this vicinity that date from the 6th century. It was once an administrative and religious centre for the Anglo Saxon kingdom of Mercia, known in those days as Hamtun. It grew in significance in Norman times when its castle and town walls were built under the stewardship of the earl, Simon de Senlis. The old defence line of the walls determined the street layout that we can still see preserved today in Bridge Street, The Drapery and Scarletwell Street. Both Henry I and Henry II held Court in Northampton on occasion.

Northampton grew during medieval times to become a manufacturing centre with a particular reputation for its production of boots and shoes. Because of this, the local soccer team would later become affectionately known as 'The Cobblers'. The town's growth was inhibited in the 16th and 17th centuries when it was ravaged by the fires of 1516 and 1675. In a way, the second disaster proved to be something of a blessing in disguise as Northampton was remodelled along spacious, well designed lines. There followed a period of rapid growth and increased prosperity in the 18th century and into the subsequent one, especially after the completion of the Grand Union Canal. This was allied with the explosion in demand for footwear and leather goods by the Army intent on equipping soldiers fighting the enemy in the Napoleonic Wars. The linking of the town with the national rail network in the mid 1840s helped complete the supply lines and Northampton boomed. Its 7,000 population in 1800 had increased 12 times over by the end of the Victorian age and it is from about that moment that our story of 'Nostalgic Northampton' begins.

We will soon turn the pages to uncover a treasure trove of memories created in part by the photographs within and in part by readers' own recollections. Some of the latter may be hazy, but they can be sharpened by looking at the evidence before their very eyes, as Arthur Askey used to put it. Many will have forgotten Phillips and Co, the game dealer on George Row, but others will fondly recall the Fifty Shilling Tailor on the edge of Market Square. There will be a chance to drink once more at the Kingsley Park Hotel or sup at the Pomfret Arms in Far Cotton as it looked in bygone times. Some may even recall being pushed in a pram bought at the establishment run by A Watts and Sons on Kettering Road. Those with a love of nostalgia will get more than a whiff of that emotion from this publication.

The companies and organisations which have developed and thrived in the area, over the recent decades, are many. The area has a proud tradition of creativity, enterprise and innovation and we take great pleasure in including in this book histories of an outstanding selection of different companies, whose contribution to the development and sustainability of the city's economic prosperity is a matter of record. With their co-operation and access to their respective photographic archives, we have been able to tell their stories. Hopefully this will trigger the memories of local people who have worked for them, or been touched by their part in community life.

Our handsome town can boast more than a few famous residents from here and we may visit some of them in our journey through time. It is the birthplace of actress Joan Hickson and England cricketer Graeme Swann. Entertainer Des O'Connor was a wartime evacuee to the town and briefly played professional football for the local team. Perhaps the reader can get in the right yesteryear mood by putting 'I Pretend', O'Connor's number one hit single from 1968, onto the Dansette record player. Now light up a Kensitas cigarette and enjoy this journey down the memory lanes of Mare Fair, Abington Street and the rest.

TEXT	ANDREW MITCHELL, STEVE AINSWORTH, TONY LAX
PHOTOGRAPH RESEARCH	TONY LAX
DESIGNER	SEAMUS MOLLOY
BUSINESS DEVELOPMENT MANAGER	STUART KIRKBY

STREET SCENES

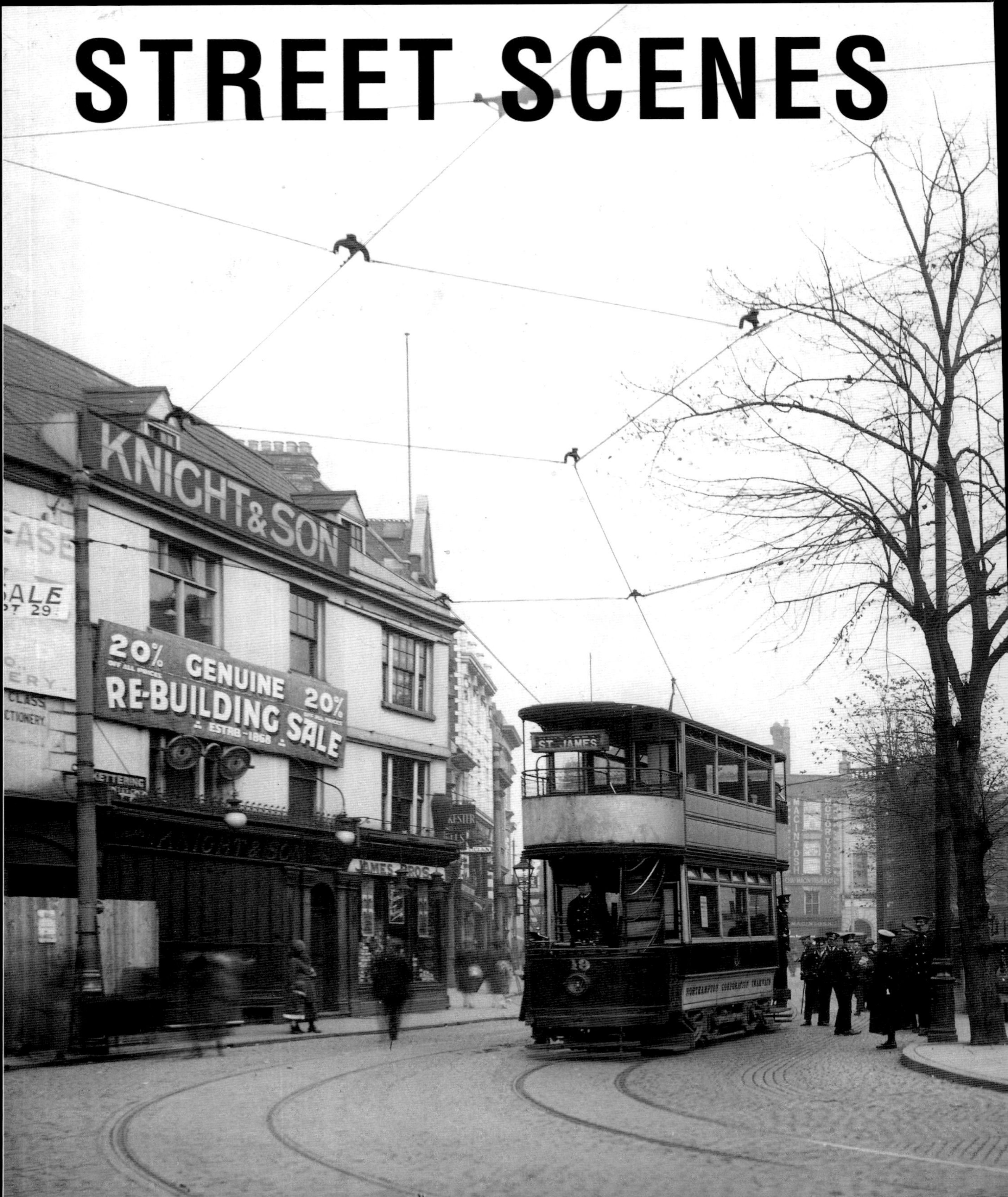

The corner with Mercer's Row and The Drapery is shown in the mid 1920s just before Knight's and Salsbury had their premises knocked down. They were to make way for a complete remodelling of this site. A new building, housing the Westminster Bank, was to appear. That fine new edifice is still with us as a financia establishment, though it has changed its ownership on several occasions in the interim. At one stage, the Anglia Building Society was based here and, more recently, it has been occupied by Nationwide. The cobbles are still in place today, but the tram heading for St James would be travelling in the wrong direction today, as traffic flow is one way along Mercer's Row towards Abington Street. The men lounging on the wall of the church remind us that this was a period of economic downturn and that many were unable to find work. The situation would only get worse as the 1930s approached.

Above: Clare Street is about half a mile from the town centre and runs from the Kettering Road junction with Talbot Road for several hundred yards until it meets Military Road, near the TA barracks (below). Looking in that direction today, the scene is little altered. We may now have Eaton House flats to the right, with Brockhall Coach Works and the Playhouse Theatre further along, but the fabric has seen little change since these late Victorian kiddies made their way to the school on the left. It was named after John Clare (1793-1864), one of the county's cultured sons despite his low birth from peasant stock. Born in Hepston, he was an influential regional poet, concentrating on celebrating rural life and bemoaning its disruption by the industrial age. His work was inhibited by bouts of alcoholism and mental illness. In more recent times, quite appropriately, the building has been used as the county's educational centre for music and the performing arts. It is a very well appointed establishment, boasting some 32 well equipped smaller rooms to supplement the three large rehearsal areas. It acts as a centre for the Associated Board (ABRSM), Trinity Guildhall and English Speaking Board exams. A number of community groups that include the Northampton Symphony Orchestra, Abington Wind Band, Northampton String Orchestra and Society of Recorder Players frequently practise at the centre.

Bottom right: Looking north from Wellingborough Road, the view is of Monks Park Road. In the distance, Percy Road and the side wall of what is now Simpson Avenue Primary School can just about be seen. The western side of the road retains its late Victorian terraced houses, if not its gas lamps. Remarkably, the quaint little porch and the house to the right on the corner of Florence Road are still very much as they were over a century ago. The wall and trees on this side have long been replaced by housing and the little girls with their dolls and pram would be hard pressed to find a safe spot to play in this street any more. The solitary horse and cart that we can observe has disappeared and lines of parked motor cars are a common feature here these days. Horse drawn vehicles clattered along streets such as this for many years after the introduction of motoring to our lives. People living in these homes could not afford such luxuries and residents were much more likely to hear the sound of hooves accompanying the milkman, coalman or totter as tradesmen came to call. The horses also left behind useful deposits that gardeners collected with shovels and buckets to take away to feed the rhubarb on their allotments. The call of 'rag-bone' rent the air more often than the pop of an exhaust pipe.

Did you know?

Northampton began as a Saxon village. It was called Hamm tun, which means the village by the well-watered meadow. Later it was called North Hamm tun.

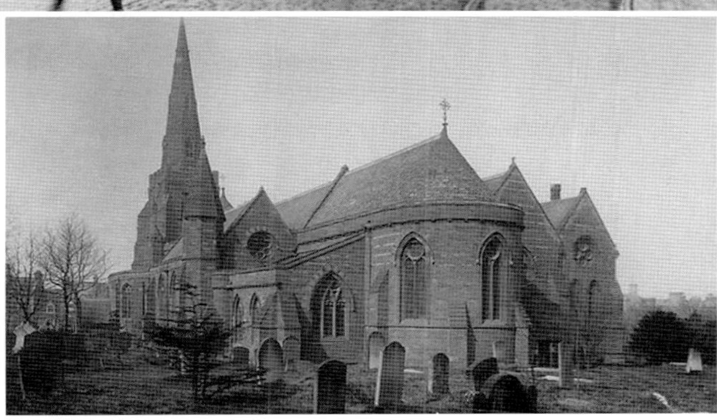

Above and left: The Church of the Sepulchre (with St Andrew and St Lawrence) is more generally known by the smaller mouthful of St Sepulchre. It was built just over 900 years ago for Simon de Senlis, Earl of Northampton, in thanks for his safe return from the Crusades. Its design was based on the original Church of the Holy Sepulchre in Jerusalem. Its spire can be seen peeking above the buildings on Sheep Street in the Edwardian scene. This thoroughfare takes its name from one of the livestock markets that were once a regular feature in this vicinity.

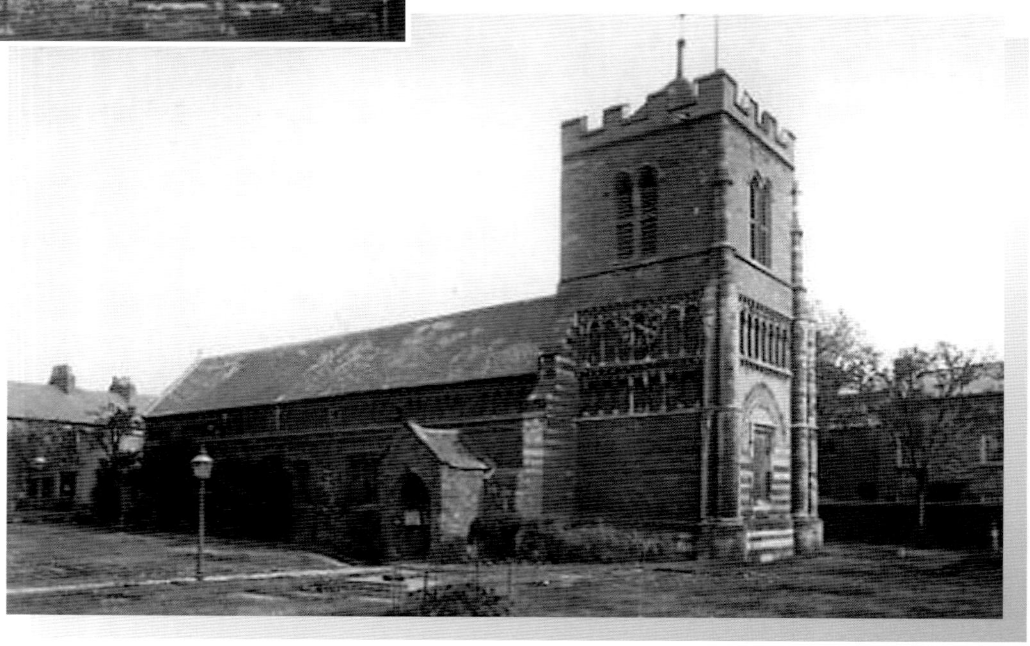

Mare Fair runs east and slightly downhill from St Peter's Way to the junction with Horse Market and Horseshoe Street. Opposite where once Charles Macquire had a pawn shop close to a barber's, The Ibis Hotel, with the Gala Casino and Rodizio's Brazilian Steak House now dominate the left hand side of the street. They lead down to what is now called Sol Centre Corner. The names of the thoroughfares in this part of town are an obvious link to the earlier times to which Daniel Defoe referred on a visit during his travels around the country. He wrote that 'This is counted the centre of all the horse markets and horse fairs in England'. The manufacture of leather goods, such as saddles, also took place in this vicinity. The photograph, from around the start of the 20th century, was taken just below St Peter's Church. This is a former Anglican building that closed as a regular religious concern in 1995. It is used on occasions for various social and community functions. Just out of shot on the right, at 33 Mare Fair, is Hazelrigg House, sometimes called Cromwell House. It is one of the town's oldest buildings, dating back to the 1570s. The house was refurbished and restored in 1988.

Billing Road runs out eastwards from the ring road around the town centre. At the time of these photographs, this was a road that featured many handsome residential properties. Quite a few of them were of considerable proportions. A lot of them are still with us, though quite a few have been converted into offices and apartments. It was along here that the General Hospital was relocated from the town centre towards the end of the 18th century on land purchased in Northampton Fields. The new building opened with 114 beds and a special wing designated as a lunatic asylum. The hospital was extended on several occasions over the years and now boasts 600 beds on a 40 acre site and employs over 4,000 staff.

The grandly named Pickering Phipps had run a small brewery in Towcester from 1801 before leasing a purpose-built one from JC Barratt in 1817. Phipps brought three of his sons, Edward, Richard and Thomas, into the business as it began to flourish. Others of his offspring prospered in farming and drapery. Pickering Phipps became Mayor of Northampton in 1821 and was still involved in Council work when he died in 1830, aged just 58. The brewery was run by successive generations of the family before being taken over by Watney Mann in 1960. Its last real ale draught beer was brewed in 1968 and a final keg version of Phipps' pale ale was drawn off in 1970. The Bridge Street premises closed in 1974 and, eventually, Carlsberg assumed the business reins and built a modern brewery on the land. The Phipps name is still used on a number of beers, so here's a cheer to the memory of Pickering Phipps and his fine ales.

The Pomfret Arms, on Cotton End, just off Old Towcester Road, was just one of many pubs that were part of the Phipps Brewery empire. The photographs are about a century apart in their age, with the group of intrepid locals aboard the dray being snapped in about 1875. The Far Cotton district has been hit by flooding a number of times over the years as it is so close to the river. The Pomfret Arms was first mentioned in a trade directory in 1830. The passageway to its side was used for carriers' carts and the headroom was too low to enable it to offer facilities to the horse drawn coaches that made their way past here in Victorian times. In any case, the pub was too small to cater for such a trade, so it existed as a simple hostelry right through the 19th and 20th centuries and into the present one. It was named after Thomas Fermor, the 4th Earl of Pomfret (1770-1833). He was a soldier in the Peninsula War and was promoted to the rank of major-general in 1813. The River Nene now approaches Northampton town from the west, passing between the southern suburbs of St. James (locally known as Jimmy's End) and Far Cotton. The Nene's third northern source, the Naseby Source or Brampton Nene, converges at the Carlsberg Brewery. The town centre of Northampton lies on the northern slope of the Nene Valley and escapes the river's flooding. However, the Far Cotton and St. James areas of the town occupy the flood plain and have borne the brunt of severe flooding over the years, culminating in the 1998 Easter floods. The picture above clearly shows a similar problem from over a hundred years earlier.

Below and right: All Saints is Northampton's parish church and a religious building has been situated in this part of town, on The Drapery, flanked by Mercer's Row and George Row, since medieval times. Not unlike the great fire of 1666 in London, the effects of Northampton's equivalent disaster in 1675 saw the town renewed architecturally. Henry Bell, a King's Lynn man resident in Northampton, was given the job of designing the new All Saints. He drew part of his inspiration from the example set by Christopher Wren who had been responsible for creating the many fine replacement buildings and churches in London. The central tower and crypt had survived the fire, so Bell set to work creating the new All Saints to the east of the tower in an almost square design. This mirrors, to quite a degree, the look of St Mary-at-Hill, one of the first of the churches for which Wren provided the blueprint. A visitor to All Saints cannot fail to be impressed by the architecture. On entering the barrel vaulted nave, one delights at the central dome, supported on four Ionic columns, that is handsomely lit by a lantern above. The church boasts a celebrated choir that can also trace its heritage to the Middle Ages. There are several divisions of singers, including a boys' section, one for girls and another for male choral scholars. In recent times, there have been singing tours to various parts of Europe and the United States. As all performers say after a 'gig', CDs are available in the foyer.

Right: The tram lines and cabling for the electrified tram system had not long been in service when this photograph on the edge of Mercer's Row was taken in the middle of the first decade of the last century. It was obviously late in the autumn or early in the winter from what we can see of the leafless trees and warmly dressed pedestrians. You can also tell that this was a long time ago because here is a uniformed bobby going about his duty. When did you last see one of those out and about on his own? All Saints Church, formerly All Hallows, has links with Norman times. However, the present building dates from the late 17th century, after the Great Fire of 1675 that gutted much of the town. King Charles II contributed 1,000 tons of timber towards the reconstruction, perhaps partly as some form of atonement for his sanctioning the destruction of Northampton castle in 1660. The rebuilt church was consecrated in 1680 and a portico and statue of King Charles added in the early 1700s. The royal connection with the church is still acknowledged on Oak Apple Day when the choir sings a Latin hymn in his memory. Since 2009, part of the church has been leased out as a coffee shop.

Did you know?

Northampton was destroyed by fire in both 1516 and 1675, and was rebuilt as a spacious and well-planned town.

Two rare views at the corner of Gold Street and Horseshoe Street. The view today would be looking across from the Vue Cinema and Ibis Hotel. Vint's Palace opened on 22 September, 1913, after Mr Leon Vint, a pioneer of cinematography, took over the lease.The venture did not last long and some six years later the premises were re-opened as the Majestic Cinema. In 1952, A. Bell & Sons opened a shop there. The early history of the building is both fascinating and colourful. A tavern of low repute by the name of The Crow and Horseshoe stood on the site for many years in the 1800s. It later changed to Thomas's New Music Hall and from October 1869 it became known as the Alhambra, which soon gained a notorious reputation for the quantity of drink consumed there. Ironically a Temperence establishment, the British Workman No1, replaced the music hall in 1877. J. Grose's cycle factory occupied the site during the late 1890s, until they were re-opened as the Palace of Varieties. In 1912, fifteen days after the New Theatre in Abington Street opened, the building was transformed into the Picture House cinema. Within a year Vint had taken over the premises.

Did you know?

Northampton Castle (now only remaining as a rebuilt postern gate in a wall outside the railway station and the hill on which it stood) was for many years one of the country's most important castles. The country's parliament sat here many times and Thomas Becket was imprisoned here until he escaped.

Northampton's oldest standing building, the Church of The Holy Sepulchre is one of the largest and best-preserved round churches in England. It was built in 1100 on the orders of the first Earl of Northampton.

VINT'S PALAC
ALWAYS AN
UP TO THE MINUTE
PROGRAM
MILK

Above and below: George Row leads past the side of All Saints Church, with the turning into Wood Hill to the left, from where the bus in the more modern picture is travelling. With the Guildhall in the distance, the Sessions House is the main point of interest to the right. Now a tourist information centre, it was the town's former administrative centre. Following the disastrous fire of 1675 that destroyed the modest timber building that once stood here, work commenced on providing Northampton with a more suitable legal heart. Designed by Henry Bell, a future Mayor of King's Lynn, its large windows allowed plenty of daylight to get into the

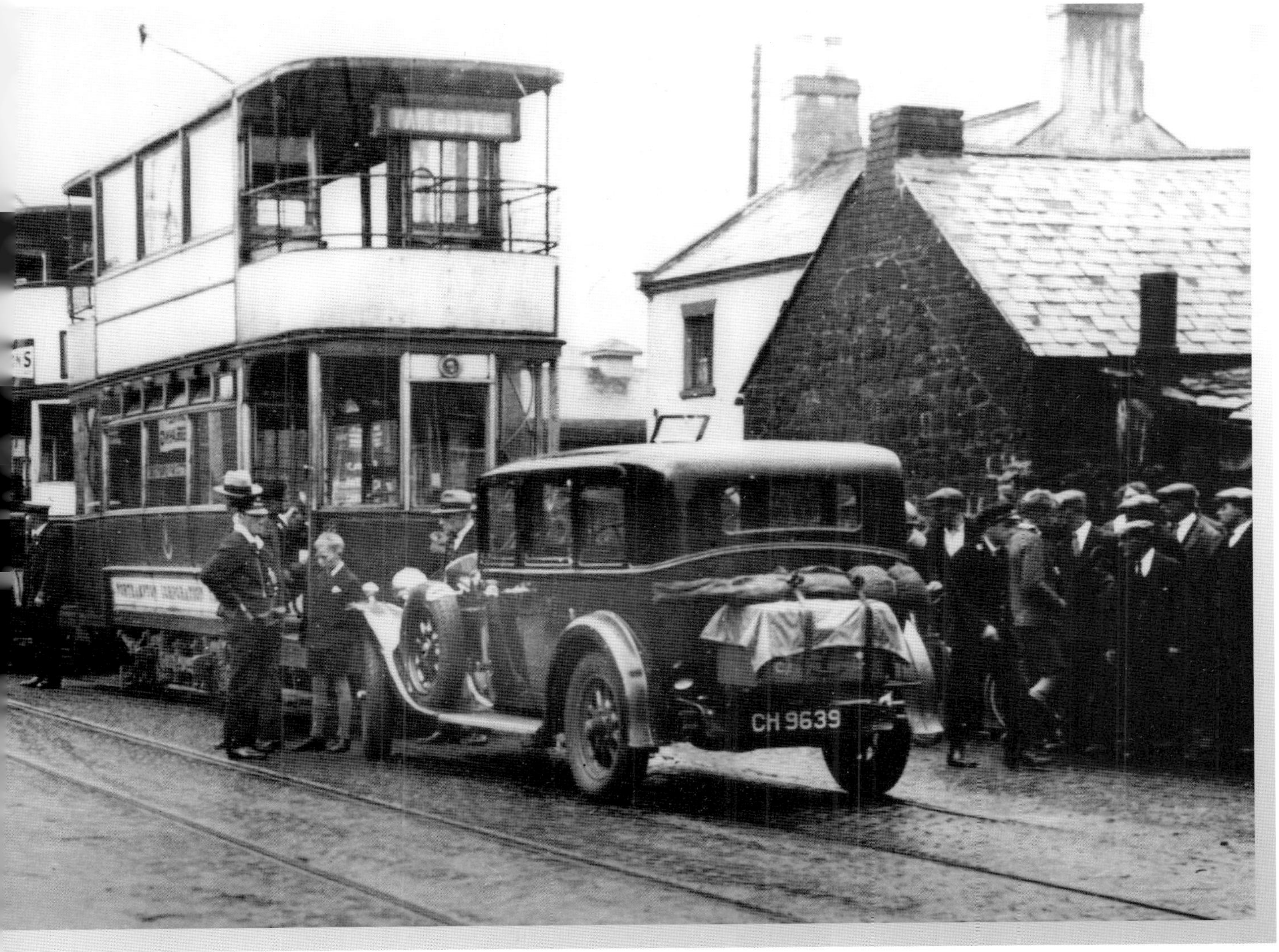

building. The £1,800 it cost to build was raised from taxation and levies. Until underfloor heating was added in the 19th century, the courtroom would have been a chilly place in which to be. Even so, many trials held here attracted good sized crowds who enjoyed the spectacle and were not averse to making the proceedings a little rowdy at times. It was here that, in 1705, two women were found guilty of witchcraft and hanged. They were the last people in the country to be executed for such a crime. The Sessions House also saw occasional use as a concert hall, market and theatre. In the older photograph, the entrance to County Hall is to the right of the Sessions House. Next to this, with a pillared porch, is the former Infirmary that was based here from 1744 to 1793, before moving to Billing Road.

Above: Passions ran high during the General Strike of 1926. A meeting of the TUC at the beginning of May declared its stand against any attempt to reduce miners' wages and increase their hours. These workers stuck to the slogan, 'Not a penny off the pay, not a minute on the day'. Workers in key areas such as transport, the shipyards, iron and steel industries, printing and building were called out with almost immeciate effect Others followed suit later. Bridge Street, one of the main routes out of town, leading to the London road, saw one of many confrontations during this difficult time. Here, at Cotton End, a car driver announced his solidarity for railway workers and their fellows. It was a rare sign of middle class solidarity with the working classes. Strikers were annoyed that trams were still running in defiance of the strike and a crowd of them was keen to 'encourage' the drivers and conductors to halt their journeys. Passengers were urged to continue their journeys on foot, which many did as they had little alternative. The strike lasted well into June, but miners continued with their action long after the rest of the country had returned to work. Eventually, most were forced back by the need to put food on the table. Relationships between them and their bosses continued to be strained and these groups remained suspicious of each other for generations.

Wood Hill, viewed either side of the last war, has seen some alterations to the facades of the buildings here. However, it still retains its place as a link between Mercer's Row and George Row, running to the rear of All Saints. The older photograph, with its blend of a horse and cart, men in flat caps and motor cars, shows how that period offered a balance of old and new, the established and the developing. In the picture from c1950 we get a far more forward-looking feeling. The fashion sense of both sexes is light and bright and the vehicles have a more modern look to them. The Black Boy Hotel at 5 Wood Hill is no more, but Oliver Adams' bakery on the corner continues to trade.

Above and below: The photographs are linked with the time when Abington Street was widened. The area then under development now includes the Skipton Building Society premises at 2 Abington Street, with a large phone shop on the opposite corner at the opening into Market Square. Bradshaw Stores and Waterloo House were later demolished, though the latter name was retained for an office block built there instead. In more modern times, Paddy Power and Mace grocery were among the ground floor retail occupants. The other photo shows the building to the right that was erected in 1940 and is now home to Leopold's Belgian chocolate and coffee house, First Choice and Caffé Nero. The building on the corner of Dychurch Lane, where a man was precariously perched on the roof ready to start the demolition process, has been replaced by one housing Thomson Travel, the Coventry Building Society and an O2 phone shop. Doffman's was an important name in the town as it was at this corner with Market Square that many older readers will recall arranging to meet sweethearts before heading off for a night out at a dance hall or cinema. The Doffman brothers were superior tailors who established one of the most successful Jewish retail outlets here in c1900. Saul and Hyman Doffman hailed from Leicester originally, but became prominent Northampton figures. Saul held a number of important civic positions during the interwar years and Hyman represented the town on the Board of Deputies of British Jews.

The Drapery is the name generally given to the whole of the street that runs from the corner of Gold Street to the junction with Greyfriars, where the building that is now home to Cancer Research UK still stands. In this collection of images we are looking in that direction, to the north from All Saints Church. In truth, The Drapery should really only be applied to the west side of the road as the opposite length is The Glovery, but the latter term has largely been forgotten. Both words, of course, aptly relate to the businesses that thrived in this area in former times. Notable traders along here at one time included E E Freedman at 15 The Drapery, in between what are now McDonald's and Oxfam. He was a tailor and benefactor in

the late Victorian age. Frederick Adnitt, the town's mayor in 1900, had a flourishing drapery business where Debenham's built its postwar store. Boots' the chemist, opposite All Saints, was formerly the place where Philadelphus Jeyes opened for business in 1810 and went on to develop his famous cleaner and disinfectant, Jeyes' Fluid. The large building on the corner with Mercer's Row was built for the Westminster Bank in the mid 1920s. Local masons, White and Joyce, provided the stonework. The copper dome, with its 45 foot circumference, can be seen from many quarters in the town. Across from there, on the other side of The Drapery, H Samuel continues to trade from this same outlet. Looking up the road today we would only see a limited number of vehicles, as there are traffic restrictions now in place.

Did you know?

Street names such as Mercer's Row, The Drapery and Woolmonger Street, derive from the main industry in medieval Northampton, which was wool making.

Northampton's Market Square, one of the largest in England, dates from 1235 when the selling of goods, including livestock, in the All Saints churchyard was stopped by King Henry III, and transferred to the Square. Livestock continued to be sold in the market until 1873, when a purpose-built cattle market opened.Prior to this, animals were penned and sold on the Market Square and the surrounding streets – hence the names of Sheep Street and Mare Fair. In 1863 a cast iron fountain was presented to the town by a Captain Isaacs to commemorate the marriage of Prince Albert (later King Edward VII) to Princess Alexandra of Denmark. The fountain stood until 1962. During the last war, tunnels under the square were opened and used as air-raid shelters. And it has been the scene of many great celebrations and ceremonial occasions, including jubilee proclamations and the VE day celebrations of 1945. The backdrop to the Market Square are the buildings which give an impression of solidity and permanence. It's hard to imagine only six years later they were gone and this aspect of the Square had changed dramatically. The buildings each had an individual style and character, having been built at different times. In 1972 the row, including Abel's Records, the Emporium Arcade, with a wonderful frontage of two-tone brickwork, and the 'Chronicle & Echo' and 'Mercury & Herald' offices were demolished to make way for the Grosvenor Shopping Centre. completely changing the character of this end of Market Square. For many local people an outing to the market would have been not just a shopping trip, but a social occasion and a chance to meet friends and have a gossip.

Did you know?

The Mercury is one of the oldest newspapers still in circulation. First published in 1720, it is the fifth-oldest newspaper in the UK and the tenth-oldest in the world.

Left: The wartime blackout came to an end just before Christmas in 1944. By then, the aerial threat from the Luftwaffe with its nighttime raids on our towns, factories and heavy industries was all but over. For more than five years we had struggled to get around once dusk came. The warden's cries of 'Turn that light out; don't you know there's a war on' would, at long last, be consigned to history and the variety halls. The blackout was introduced at the start of hostilities and an almost complete ban on showing any light was rigorously enforced. Here, everyone in and around Market Square at the bottom of Abington Street and Wood Hill, turned on every light that they possibly could. The dark and gloomy times had ended and a bright future lay ahead, or so they thought in 1945.

Gold Street is one of the oldest parts of the town. It runs from what used to be Boot's corner at the Drapery out to Horse Market at the spot now known as Sol Centre. The street names in and around the town centre reflect the trades and activities that were often carried out in these localities. An early financial centre was established within the Gold Street area by one particular group who set up an early form of banking facility. Back in the 13th century, Northampton had a significant Jewish population, centred on this part of town.

Nearly 300 Jews were executed in 1277, accused of coin clipping, and those living here were largely driven out of town in the sort of purge that would be recreated in different countries across Europe in succeeding centuries. Some of the history of this street was uncovered quite recently when workmen dug up the road at the start of 2007 to lay a new water main. Remnants of a medieval street were discovered, providing links back to Saxon times. More recent artefacts were also found, especially pieces of leather stuck in the Victorian drains. This set of photographs shows scenes from the second quarter of the 20th century. The earliest includes a policeman on point duty. This used to be a regular sight at road junctions in most town centres. The introduction of electrically-controlled traffic lights in some places did away with the need to have guardians of the law controlling traffic, but the bobby continued to be a common sight at other busy intersections up to and into the final quarter of the 1900s. Times change and a number of famous businesses, such as the T C Palmer fashion store and Woolworths 'five and dime' shop, have not survived.

The images on these two pages look at Abington Street over the years. One the facing page is an elevated view looking east from Market Square finds the street thronged with shoppers. Fashions and vehicles indicate the 1950s and the numbers of people about suggest a time of day when, only a few years later, the traffic would be nose-to-tail down the street. These were calmer times, however, as far as cars were concerned and freer movement was allowed after the bottleneck which had blighted the street had been demolished in 1946. The site on the corner of Dychurch Lane, to the right of the photograph, had not yet been developed when this picture was taken. Much of the interest in the picture lies on the right-hand side. Above Wiggins & Co Ltd is a round sign indicating the offices of Friends Provident and Century Insurance. This has a splendidly solid and old-fashioned ring about it, but it is the nostrils of the older readers which might quiver at the mention of Kingham's Grocers. This, too, was to be found in the block of buildings to the right and is best remembered for the aroma of roasting coffee which wafted out of it and along Abington Street. It is still one of the busiest retail areas in Northampton. In more modern times the street has been closed to traffic, from the corner with Drychurch Lane right through to St Giles Terrace. Shoppers can now happily promenade along the pedestrianised area without having to keep a wary lookout for the many cars and buses that used to crowd their way along here. Although the town has its malls and shopping centres, it is good that there is still a balance. Along Abington Street there is still plenty of choice to be had as the shops are varied and, in some cases, specialist. Traditional stalls in Market Square also offer a variety and are within east reach of here.

Did you know?

Northampton was designated a New Town in the United Kingdom in 1968, and the Northampton Development Corporation (NDC) was set up to almost double the size of the town.

INC.
SITE

Below: On the corner with Conduit Lane, a long line mainly comprised of housewives stretched around from Mercer's Row. Smith's ironmongery, under the County Café, had not attracted such large numbers to buy the Two Ronnies' four candles or 'Os' as it was next door upon which interest was centred. This scene was captured at a time when rationing was at its height. Clothing joined the list of commodities for which you had to have coupons before making a purchase and a rumour had spread that Lyons had just received a delivery of clothes that were off ration. They arrived in droves hoping that the tale was true. It was not surprising that people were desperate to get their hands on goods that had been in short supply since the summer of 1941. Initially, an adult was allowed 60 coupons per annum, though this was later reduced to 48. Since a dress used up 11 coupons and it was 8 for a shirt, the allowance did not go far when you started buying underwear and the occasional jacket. Spivs and black marketers loved the situation, as did GIs with their pockets stuffed full of nylon stockings to tempt women into parting with something other than just their cash. Clothes remained on ration until 1949, but certain foodstuffs, such as tea, sugar and sweets, stayed on the list until the early 1950s.

Right: Many readers may still remember the old junction of the Harborough and Welford Roads before the road pattern was changed in the early 1960s. Although there are some fairly 'antique' vehicles in the garage forecourt to the right, the presence of a Morris Minor heading towards the town centre probably places this picture in the late 1950s. Accustomed as we are to large, very readable green signs at major junctions, the little old black and white signs seem piffling in comparison, easily missed at night or in poor visibility. The name 'Cleveland' should evoke some memories for those who were motorists in this era, along with the distinctively shaped petrol pump tops. No such thing as self-service pumps in those days. You were likely to be served by somebody wiping their hands on an oily rag who would have given you a very funny look if you had asked for crisps and chocolates as well! It was a nice touch to thank customers in such a prominent way, but the garage was to disappear in the changes to come. Cleveland was Esso's secondary brand, famous for marketing a petrol-alcohol blend called Discol. Soon after 1972 the brand was eliminated and alcohol blended fuel disappeared from the UK market.

Below right: A view along St Giles Street looking from The Guildhall, probably from the late 50s, with Derngate off to the right. Prominent in shot are the Prudential Buildings, with Montague Jeffery Menswear Shop on the corner. For more than 110 years, Montague Jeffery has been synonymous with quality meanswear in the East Midlands. In the Autumn of 1901, Harold Montague Jeffery, opened a business at premises in Wood Hill, next to McKinnell's the Chemists. Initially trading as a Hosier and Hatter, it was from this beginning that the comprehensive gentlemen's outfitting shop we see today developed. In 1923, when the lease expired in Wood Hill, the firm moved for a short time to a shop adjacent to the Town Hall at 3 St. Giles Street and in 1928, Montague's only son, Bernard, joined his father in business. It was not long after this that plans for the widening of St Giles Street were implemented and the parade of shops which now stands on the corner of St. Giles Street and Derngate was rebuilt. Today, looking along St Giles Street, past the Post Office, all the cars would be facing you, as the traffic flow is all one-way down the street.

ENTERTAINMENT, LEISURE & PASTIMES

Below: Can you imagine giant brown bears, performing in your local street, not in a cage or well away from fascinated onlookers, but within feet of young children? Health and safety and animal cruelty regulations would never allow this to take place these days, but during the Victorian age it was a different story, as can be seen in this image from Gold Street in 1906. In many principal thoroughfares throughout the country, daily life would come to a standstill as the street entertainers came to town. Dancing bears were just one of many popular acts, townsfolk may also have seen poor wretches singing songs, telling jokes, or imitating birds or animals for a few pennies. The bears, were usually of Russian origin and made to dance or perform tricks before begging for food from the crowd. Even at the time, not everyone was happy with events and the Secretary of State for the Home Department was asked whether he could take steps to stop future performances.

Did you know?

In his 18th century 'Tour through the Whole Island of Great Britain', Daniel Defoe described Northampton as "...the handsomest town in all this part of England."

Above: A travelling circus advertised its presence in the town with a parade of stiltwalkers, clowns, tumblers, jugglers and a family of elephants. One trader in Market Square was less than happy to see Nellie and her companions as they raided his wares, consuming a barrowload of produce that he could ill afford to lose. The buildings in the background include one used by Church's China and Glass Company. This is one of Northampton's longest running businesses, serving the town for about 150 years. It was set up by Thomas Church in 1858 when he took over premises in Devizes. With the assistance of son Wesley, the firm came to Northampton in the early 1870s. Wesley married Sarah Spencer a shoemaker's daughter, and they set up both shop and home in Parade House, a former hotel on the north side of Market Square. Successive generations of the family ran the business until the founder's great grandson, Vivian, took over the other side of the front of the Arcade as well in the 1960s. A move was made to Welsh House on the square in 1975, before relocating to St Giles Street in 1996 when a 3,500 square feet store was opened; Lord Wedgwood presiding at the ceremony.

Below: The stuffed boxing kangaroo was something of a talking point in the bar of the Two Brewers Inn at 25 Abington Street. Well, it would have been once over for the landlord and his customers in the early 1900s when it first appeared looming large by the mirror, but after a while it became just another piece of furniture. Some drinkers saw pink elephants, but a boxing kangaroo was something else. A haunt of the theatrical profession, it became well known for its 400-500 framed photographs of theatrical and music hall artists and rather unusually, a stuffed kangaroo in the bar. Publican Clarke, a former music hall artist, claimed to have toured the world twice with his animal act and his boxing kangaroo. Pubs in the past quite often had specimens from the world of taxidermy. However, they tended to be pheasants, hare, fish and other game trophies. Around the turn into the last century, one of the licensees at the Two Brewers, Leo Clarke, had been quite well known in the area as a showman. In the 1890s he had a series of animal acts with which he used to entertain the public. The boxing kangaroo was one of its highlights. Animal acts were very popular in variety halls and with travelling fairs and circuses. When Leo's kangaroo threw its last punch, he bought the Two Brewers, had his old pal stuffed and raised on a shelf above the heads of his customers.

Top right: The River Nene rises at Arbury Hill, the county's highest point, before flowing some 88 miles until it reaches The Wash. It runs through the southern suburbs of our town at St James and Far Cotton. The river's name has been spelt 'Neen', 'Nenn' and 'Nyn' at various times in the past, before settling on the current usage in late Victorian times. However, pronunciation still varies, the long 'ee' or short 'e' sounds being used in different parts of the shire. In the photograph keen, if slightly bored looking, anglers were hoping for a catch. There was little in the way of commercial traffic to disturb their sport, so they could happily cast away to their hearts' content. Knowledgeable fishermen looked for chub and dace along the Northampton stretch, while those after carp tended to head for Ringstead Shallows, over to the east. Now, where's that landing net?

Below: Two different scenes of how it used to look as we take a stroll around the open area we now know as Becket's Park. The railings on the right enclosed land that was then known as Cow Meadow and there may be some senior citizens who remember Friesian cows grazing there. The early picture is looking along Victoria Walk, past Thomas Becket's well, alongside the A428 Bedford Road. The young ladies in the bottom picture, offer friendly smiles as they perambulate along Paradise Walk in 1937. The picture was taken from the bottom of Cheyne Walk, looking towards Bedford Road, and is evocative in so many ways. The railings have been removed and the asphalt path replaced by grass. The cooling tower to the right belonged to the Hardingstone Junction Power Station, and was later joined by two others. They have all since been demolished. One intriguing part of this 1937 scene is to see a man pushing a pram - quite unusual for that era. But back to the young ladies. Paradise Walk was clearly a lovely place to stroll and chat whilst taking baby on an outing, and possibly these were nannies.

Left: The youngsters were fascinated by the sight of a soldier on guard duty, dressed in his regimental best and sporting a fine bearskin. They might have seen photographs of someone who looked very similar standing to attention outside Buckingham Palace, but never in front of All Saints Church. Whether or not the kiddies were heading for a pew inside is doubtful. The sheer novelty of the soldier standing so still would keep them occupied for quite a while. He was Guardsman John Turland of the Inkerman Company of Grenadier Guards and in town as part of a recruitment drive. At about the same time, in c1960, a service was being held to mark one of the periodic openings of Northampton Assizes. First connected with the town in 1176, these courts were held from time to time until they, along with Quarter Sessions, were abolished in England and Wales in the early 1970s and replaced by Crown Courts. Northampton Castle acted as the seat of the Assizes for several hundred years before falling into disrepair. A levy was made on the people of the town in the 1670s and funds raised provided for the Sessions House on George Row that would be a centre of administration for the next three centuries. A tourist and information centre is now to be found there.

Did you know?

A University of Northampton was established in 1261 by scholars from the University of Cambridge. It briefly flourished, but was dissolved by Henry III in 1265. Apparently, it posed a threat to the University of Oxford.

Left: The first York Brothers passenger coach was described as the 'criterion of luxury design'. The brothers, George and Frederick York, with initial help from their father, Anderson, expanded the original small carrier company into a larger business with a grand fleet of touring buses. As the firm expanded it took over several smaller companies, such as Law's, Knight's and Abbott's, either side of the last war. It also set up a travel company to augment its trade. During the 1939-45 war, excursions were abandoned because of petrol rationing. York Brothers used its fleet instead to ferry munitions workers to and from their places of employment and, in the early part of the hostilities, to carry the scores of children evacuated to the area from London. It is possible that a young Des O'Connor was carried on such a vehicle when he came to Northampton from Stepney as a schoolboy at this time. This line of coaches was waiting to take Co-operative workers on a staff excursion in c1949. The happy, smiling faces we can see through the windows suggest that this was going to be a really good day out. The drivers were soon to be behind the wheel and they knew that they were guaranteed a whip round at the end of the excursion, preceded by a few choruses of 'For he's a jolly good fellow.'

Below: Carrying the little case that so epitomised the sort of hand luggage people used in c1935 and into the 1940s, the woman in the middle of the group looked on as a booking was made for a trip on a coach to Great Yarmouth. A very smartly turned out lady at her side was amused by the antics of the terrier, though everyone else was more concerned about seeing which coach they were on. Journey by 'chara', as the coach was popularly known, was in its heyday either side of the last war. Most people could not afford a family saloon, so the motor car did not come into its own until the start of the 1960s. Transport for a day at the seaside or a trip into the countryside was provided by any of a number of bus companies that flourished at this time.

Abington Park has lakes, aviaries, a bandstand and a museum, as well as trees and open areas of grassland and is Northampton's most popular park. Created by the Thursby family in the late 17th century, it was given to the people of Northampton by Lady Wantage in 1892 and opened to the public in 1897. Two years later, Abington Museum was opened in the centre of the park. it was the first public park in the town and is one of its most important assets. Set within the park are the ruins of the former village of Abington and the medieval manor house, mentioned in the Domesday Book in 1086. In the upper park the 15th century manor house is now a museum. Once the home of Shakespeare's granddaughter, Elizabeth Bernard, the museum features displays depicting the whole of life in Northamptonshire. In the picture above mother, or possibly nanny, was pushing her charge in the pram as they both enjoyed the sunshine in Abington Park. The other youngster was having a whale of a time in his toy car, pushing it along for all he was worth. No doubt, he scuffed the toecaps of his shoes trying to get up a little speed. That did not matter because he was a lad. You were allowed to have boys' pastimes and ones that were just for girls in those distant times. In the unisex generation sugar and spice has had to join forces with who must never own up to preferring dolls to other toys. Nor must it admit to getting fun out of shooting a potato gun.

Above: The sun always seemed to shine when we were young. What grand times we had, just messing about in parks and open spaces. We ran across the grass playing 'tig' and 'catch me if you can'. There were jolly games of hide and seek and, if someone had brought along a few simple items of equipment, then a mass game of cricket, rounders or football could be enjoyed. On arrival at the boating lake at Abington Park, we took off our socks and shoes and paddled away contentedly. Naughty boys in their rowing boats splashed their oars so that the girls' dresses got wet through. Mums dished out perilous warnings about 'catching our deaths', but who ever got pneumonia from a few drops of water? Abington Park is still the town's most popular open space. The boating lake was repaired and its banks and paths refurbished in 2002.

This page: There was a time before the computer age when teenagers went out and about for their amusement. They went to a youth club where they could participate in games that took intelligence to play and provided an outlet for sensible conversation. It was also a good place to have the pleasant company of the opposite sex and enjoy jiving to records (remember them?) playing on a turntable. With Buddy Holly belting out 'Oh Boy' or Eddie Cochran urging 'C'mon Everybody', we demonstrated our neat steps across the floor as we impressed our partners with our dancing skills. Young people could enjoy a night out fortified by a couple of glasses of Tizer or Coca-Cola. Northampton Roadmenders Youth Club on Lady's Lane was a place offering happy and healthy times to the teens of yesteryear. The original club was opened by Earl Spencer on Lawrence Street in 1934. It has also been used as a sporting facility and community hall. Now called simply Roadmender, the venue has been a centre for live music since the 1980s. Touring bands such as Coldplay, Radiohead, Oasis and Pulp have all played here. With support from Northampton Council and the Arts Council, Roadmender has also featured contemporary dance, theatre and the visual arts.

Right: Either a forerunner of Lloyd Bridges in TV's 'Sea Hunt' or a throwback to Johnny Weissmuller as Tarzan, this intrepid diver attracted a number of admirers at the Midsummer Meadow baths. The Northampton Town and County Grammar School enjoyed use of the facility that, because of its name, might have had some in the future wondering about John Nettles investigating a series of murders. Happily, there was no jiggery pokery during this visit in the 1950s by boys from a school that can date its roots back to Tudor times. After several incarnations in and around the town, a site was eventually found in 1911 on Billing Road. Some eyebrows were lifted by traditionalists when girls were admitted to the Sixth Form in the 1990s. By then, the lads lounging at the poolside had moved on to a variety of careers. Notable old boys include journalist Ray Gosling, G R James, the Bishop of Norwich, and composer Trevor Hold. The outdoor swimming pool, situated in this large recreational area close to the River Nene, was especially popular either side of the last war. It had opened in 1908, but numbers declined in the latter years of the 20th century and it was demolished in 1983.

Did you know?

Walter Tull, Northampton Town FC player became Britain's first black army officer in the First World War.

Des O'Connor, television presenter and singer, was evacuated to the town in 1932 during WWII and briefly played for Northampton Town FC.

Below: No football fan likes to see their team being beaten, but in the 5th round FA Cup tie on 7 February, 1970, did Northampton Town supporters witness a performance of class and skill from the 'best player in the world'? George Best returned from a six-week suspension - imposed after he threw mud at the referee during an international - and took out all his frustrations on the Cobblers, scoring six of Manchester United's goals in an 8-2 drubbing. Unfortunately, although talented, some of our players were unable to cope with his world class skills on the day. Even Northampton fans and players could appreciate the full range of his ability and devastating finishing. Northampton deserved the two goals that came their way, however, the day belonged to 'El Beatle'. It is likely that goalie Kim Book had backache by the end, but a place in history was assured.

Right: Charles Bradlaugh was a political activist and one of the most famous English atheists of the 19th century. He was an advocate of trade unionism, republicanism, and women's suffrage, and he opposed socialism. He wrote a series of pamphlets on politics and religion and by the early 1860s was recognised as one of the leading freethinkers in Britain. In 1880 Bradlaugh was elected Member of Parliament for Northampton, but because of his initial refusal to take the religious 'Oath of Allegiance', he effectively forfeited his seat. After several subsequent attempts to take the oath, one of which saw him imprisoned in the Tower of London, he eventually succeeded and took his seat in the House of Commons. Bradlaugh died on 30 January, 1891, at the age of 57. His funeral was attended by 3,000 mourners, including a then 21 years-old Mahatma Gandhi. He is buried in Brookwood Cemetery. A statue to Bradlaugh is located on a traffic island at Abington Square pointing west towards the centre of Northampton. Various local landmarks are named after Bradlaugh, including Bradlaugh Fields nature reserves, The Charles Bradlaugh pub, and Charles Bradlaugh Hall at the University of Northampton.

Below: Situated in Abington Street, the New Theatre was built by the respected theatre architect W. G. R Sprague and opened in December 1912. The auditorium seated over 2000 people, and many well-known artists appeared over the years including Dame Clara Butt, Pavlova, Gracie Fields and Max Wall. After spending a few days in London, Laurel and Hardy opened their 1953 tour at the New Theatre. They apparently stayed at the Plough Hotel, in Bridge Street. After rehearsals, they posed for photographs in Abington Street, with local schoolchildren to help promote "Road Safety Week." The last performance at the New Theatre took place on 16 August, 1958 and subsequently its contents were auctioned off, before the building was demolished in 1960. This was the same year as another of Northampton's Town Centre historical attractions was demolished; the Peacock Hotel, an ancient coaching inn built c1456. A supermarket was built on the site of the New Theatre and in more recent years, a Primark store.

Did you know?

Errol Flynn acted in the Northampton Repertory Theatre in 1933/34.

St Giles Square links St Giles Street with George Row and is blessed by the grand architecture of the Guildhall. Northampton's original Town Hall was located on the southwest corner of Abington Street, across from Market Place, but, by the middle of the 19th century, had become inadequate because of its restricted size. An architectural competition was held to provide a replacement and to develop the town centre's civic area. The new Guildhall was designed by Ernest Godwin in 1861-64. Mayor Pickering Phipps, the brewery magnate, laid the foundation stone on 22 October, 1861. A later mayor, Mark Dorman, presided at the opening ceremony. At that time, the clock tower was central to the building, but when it was extended in 1889-92 to Matthew Holding's design, it became offset. The Guildhall's Gothic grandeur is a match for any similar structure elsewhere in Europe. All Saints Church can be seen in the distance. The shops on the corner with Guildhall Road to the left have gone, opening up access to the old County Police Office. The gable end that once advertised Wills' Gold Flake is now part of ASK, an Italian restaurant. Beyond it is Mr Grant' House, named after a former Town Gaol's Governor. Built in 1840, it has various uses. As well as an overflow to the Sessions House and old Police Station, it was also used for a while as a visitor centre. The Old Bank, presently a pub, is just beyond here at 4/5 St Giles Square.

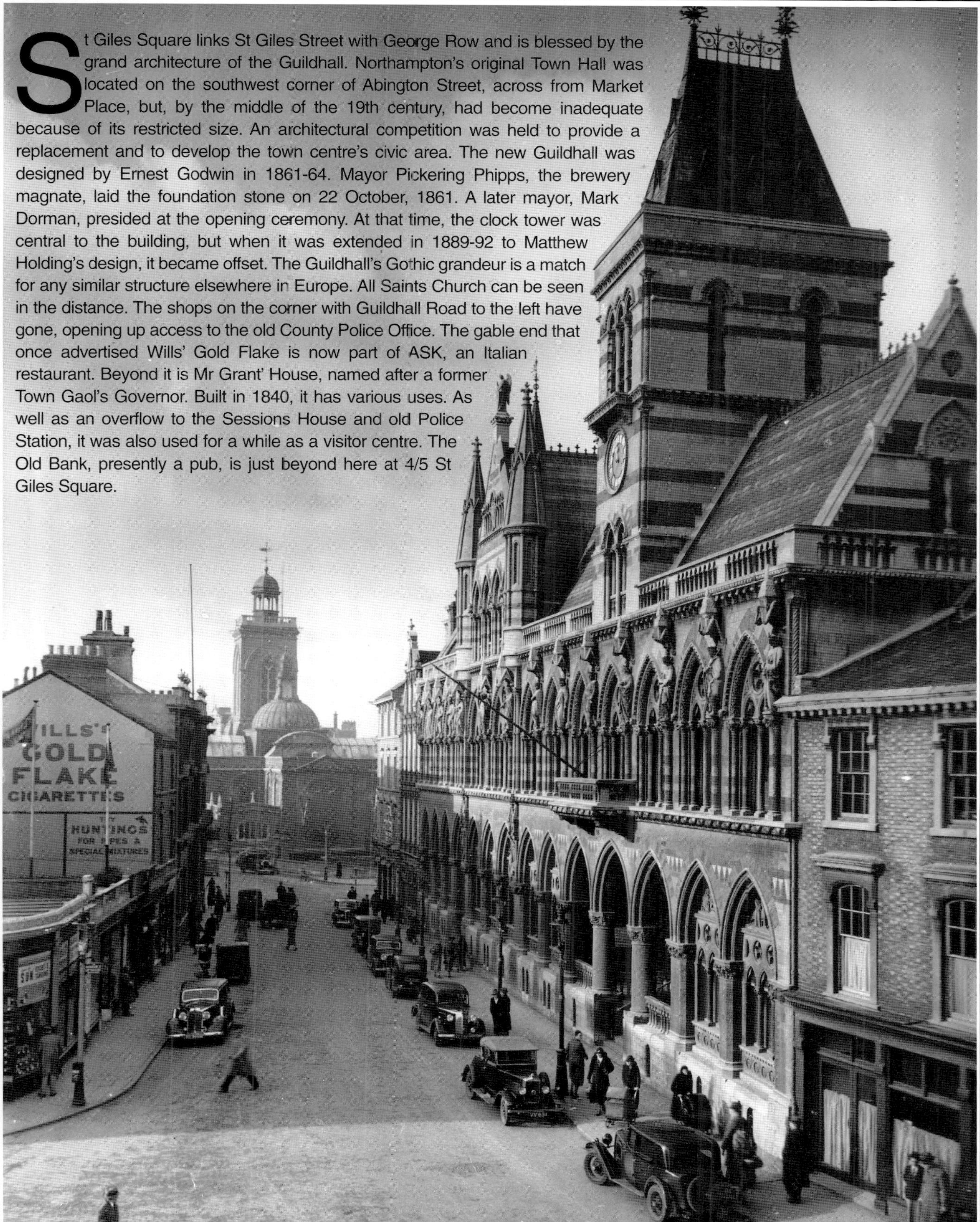

Below: An early view of how it used to look along Victoria Walk, running alongside Bedford Road, heading towards Derngate and the bottom of Cheyne Walk. On the left is Becket's park and on the right is the Grade II listed, Thomas Becket's Well. In the early 12th century Henry II often held Court in the town and Becket would have travelled along this road where it is thought he stopped to have a drink from a well on the edge of the park. During his famous fallout with the king, Becket at one time escaped from Northampton Castle through the unguarded northern gate to flee the country. At the heart of this tale, lies a personal dispute between Henry II, who felt betrayed by his friend, and Becket, who mistrusted the motives of the king. This bad blood between friends is what made the dispute so bitter. Henry claimed Thomas had stolen money from government funds. Thomas denied the charge but offered to repay the full amount regardless, to settle the argument quickly. Henry refused and demanded a trial. This led to a confrontation at Northampton Castle. On 8 October, 1164, Thomas was tried and convicted for contempt of royal authority and malfeasance whilst Lord Chancellor. Fearing the consequences, Thomas escaped and went on the run to France. In 1170 he returned to England but was assassinated soon afterwards. This violent act shocked the Christian world and ensured Thomas Becket's place in history.

Above: The village of Sulgrave is in the southwest of the county, not far from Banbury. Its main claim to fame is that it is here that a visitor can find the ancestral home of the Washington family who gave the world the first American President. Looking a little dilapidated in this photograph, Sulgrave Manor has since been restored to some of its former glory. Lawrence Washington hailed from the Lancashire area and it was he who came to Northamptonshire in the 16th century. He was twice the county town's mayor and had Sulgrave Manor built as his family home. Lawrence's great-grandson, John, emigrated to the colony of Virginia in 1656. He was a successful tobacco plantation owner and it was his own great-grandson, George, who rose to the highest office in the land after the American War of Independence. The ancestral manor house had become quite shabby by the dawning of the 20th century. A committee had been set up in 1911 in anticipation of the centenary of the 1814 Treaty of Ghent that marked the end of hostilities with America. As a further attempt to establish a special relationship with our cousins across the Atlantic, the house was purchased and restoration work begun. Patronage was provided by such luminaries as Theodore Roosevelt, Andrew Carnegie and Lord Beaverbrook. Opened to the general public in 1921 by the Marquis of Cambridge, the house and grounds became a symbol of Anglo-American co-operation.

Did you know?

Violet Gibson, would-be assassin of Benito Mussolini in 1926 is buried in Kingsthorpe and Jerome K. Jerome, author of Three Men in a Boat and other works, died in Northampton General Hospital in 1927.

Above: There were in fact twelve stone monuments erected between 1291 and 1294 in memory of Eleanor of Castile (1241-1290), wife of King Edward I marking the route of her body as it was taken to London. Queen Eleanor died at Harby near Lincoln and the King escorted the body of his wife to Westminster Cathedral. During the twelve day journey they rested each night at the locations which were subsequently marked by the monuments with a cross adourning the top. There are only three crosses remaining with two of those standing in Northamptonshire. One lies at Geddington which was on the third night of rest and one at Hardingstone which was the following night. The Geddington monument is renowned to be the best preserved of the three with the final cross standing at Waltham which is number ten of the twelve sites.

Right: Henry Compton began work on Castle Ashby House in 1574 and building continued until 1600, when Queen Elizabeth stayed in the house. King James I was a frequent guest. During the 17th century, various additions were made to Castle Ashby, notably the front façade was added by Indigo Jones. In 1688 Henry Compton, Bishop of London and uncle of the 4th Earl, found himself in conflict with the Roman Catholic King James II. He retreated to Castle Ashby and lived for two years in a secret part of the Castle, now known as the Bishop's Rooms. Later, when King James was deposed, the Castle gave refuge to Princess Anne before she was escorted to Oxford to meet her father, the new King William III. In October 1695, the King himself came to stay at Castle Ashby and personally suggested the planting of four avenues of trees opposite each face of the house. In 1760, Capability Brown provided designs for much of the parklands and built the Temple that can be seen across the menagerie pond. Castle Ashby House has recently been passed to Earl Compton, the son of the 7th Marquess, to continue the family tradition of managing the Castle Ashby Estate.

GEORGE
ALES
STOUT
COACH & HORS

A fantastic shot of the 'George Hotel', a great coaching inn which stood on the town centre, at the corner of George Row and Bridge Street. This picture shows the scale and external facade of the building in 1914. It was for several centuries the centre of many important activities in civic, social and domestic life in the town. The earliest mention of the inn appears in the minutes of the Town Assembly of 1555. The building was destroyed by the Great Fire of Northampton in 1675 and subsequently a new inn was erected on the site.The great and the good of Northampton attended events and gatherings in the large ballroom at the hotel. Even Paganini, the great violinist, performed in a concert there in 1834. After the Corn Exchange and new Town hall were built, the George began to diminish in popularity and eventually the building was sold in 1919. It was demolished in 1921 to be replaced by Lloyds Bank.

Above: The Edwardian period only lasted for just under a decade at the start of the last century, but it marked a beginning of a shift in attitudes to many elements of the British way of life. Where Queen Victoria had been insular, despite being head of a mighty empire, her son, Edward VII, was much more outward looking. As the leader of a fashionable elite, his style was influenced by the art and fashions of Europeans. There were changes afoot at home. Women began to agitate for greater equality, workers demanded better conditions and secondary education was extended to a larger number of children from poor and working class families. The kiddies playing round the market cross in the square at Higham Ferrers, a small town between Rushden and Irthlingborough, would see greater change still after the First World War when the power of the ruling classes was challenged as never before. Higham Ferrers has many fine, old buildings grouped around its centre and they form part of a conservation area. The name of Henry Chichele features heavily in the locality. He became Archbishop of Canterbury in 1414 and founded Chichele College, a training centre for secular canons. Now largely in ruins, only one hall survives. He also established the Bede House, a form of early charitable old folk's home located next to St Mary's Church.

Did you know?

The first public library in Northampton opened in 1877.

This page: Just over 118 acres in size and one of the largest landmarks in the town, the Racecourse has played a large part in local history. Races had been held on the site unofficially since 1632. In 1937, under the patronage of Lord Spencer, the first official race meet was held on the new course. These races were very popular and frequently visited by Royalty, among them the Prince of Wales, later Edward VII. With the expansion of the Racecourse came the development of the surrounding area with large houses being built for the ardent race goers. To the far side of the park is the White Elephant public house (pictured right). It started life as the Kingsley Park Hotel and was built to serve the racing fraternity. Races were not the only spectator event held on the site. From 1715 until 1818, it was used for public executions. The Jockey Club closed the site for race meetings after the deaths of some spectators and the lobbying of various groups. In 1912 the Council started to develop the area, but the outbreak of war meant it was converted into an army camp for the Welsh Division. During the Second World War the Racecourse once again was utilised as an army barracks. In 1953, when the camp was demolished Racecourse was once again brought back to become a green area with tree planting and re-landscaping.

Right: It's a lively scene of human activity in the Market Square in the 1950s. The stalls are thronged and a hand-cart awaits to help unload the contents of the wagon marked 'Tomkins Seeds.' The handsome building outside which the wagon is parked is The Peacock. This was an old coaching inn with stabling for 30 horses and a feature of the Square. As part of Northampton's heritage, it provided a link to the time when the horse was the speediest form of transport and the Market Square would echo to the sound of hooves and coach wheels on the cobbles. Unfortunately, The Peacock stood in the way of 1960s 'progress'; a time when scant regard was given to continuity and tradition in the quest for modernity. This historic building was bulldozed to make way for a featureless office block in 1961. A moderns shot from the same angle would reveal much that is different. That is to be expected of the centre of any twentieth century town or city. However, one feature provides a constant on the skyline, the impressive Town Hall tower.

Below and right: The building, branded 'Northampton's only super cinema', opened as the Savoy on 2 May, 1936. The first show starred Jack Benny in "Broadway Melody of 1936". In the 1950s ABC embarked on a programme of modernisation, the individual cinema names were dropped and they all became know as 'the ABC'. The Savoy was the first cinema in town to pioneer 3D movies in the 1950s. In 1963, the Beatles performed ten numbers on stage, culminating with 'Twist and Shout' during what can only be described as a mass frenzy of screaming fans. In 1974, the building was converted into a three-screen complex. Later, in 1986, the ABC was taken over by the Cannon Group. The Cannon closed on 27 April, 1995, with 'Pulp Fiction', 'Terminal Velocity' and 'Just Cause', as the final films. The building recognisable now as the Jesus Centre, was sympathetically restored to the glory of the 1930s by the current owners. Known as 'The Deco' from 2005, it was hired out for conferences, special events and live performances. However, this did not prove successful and it closed in July 2007. The Grade II Listed building, on the corner of Northampton's Lower Mounts, remains in church use.

A wonderful atmosphere of bustle and activity is evoked in this shot of Market Square showing an open-air market as it really should be. Masses of people are seeking that little bit of extra value for money, or even a real bargain, and you can almost hear the stallholders shouting out their special offers or exchanging banter with prospective customers. For many people in this photograph, the outing to market will have been not merely a shopping trip, but a social occasion, a chance to meet friends and have a gossip. Modern shopping centres have their advantages, but they seem anonymous and lifeless in comparison to the good old-fashioned open-air market. The busy scene pre-dates 1962, for that was the year in which the centre point of Market Square, the fountain, was dismantled. Some familiar names of the time may be seen on the premises in the background. On the left is Roses Fashion Centre, Phoenix Assurance, alongside Phelan and Agutter, Estate Agents. On the right-hand side of the Square the names of Pearl Assurance and Liptons are visible. The distinctive tower and cupola of All Saints Church dominates the skyline, with the dome of the Westminster Bank to the right.

Sight and Sound Technology

Making Life Clearer

Northampton is better known for its shoe making industry than high-tech business, but since 1979 it has been the home to Sight and Sound Technology who provide solutions and support that change the lives of those who are blind, visually impaired or have reading and learning difficulties.

Today, based at Welton House, Moulton Park, Northampton, Sight and Sound Technology, is the UK's leading provider of hardware and software to the blind, visually impaired and those with learning and reading difficulties. The company works in unison with private individuals, charitable organisations, educational establishments and commercial enterprises to help its users fully realise their potential. Products have been specifically designed to improve quality of life at work, at study or in the home.

A commitment to continual product refinement and innovation means that Sight and Sound Technology's solutions are the best available. What's more, they're simple to set up and easy-to-use.

Sight and Sound Technology is a nationwide company. Locating its Head Office in Northampton enables it to provide its customers with responsive training and support at the location of the end-user. Trained staff visit users in their home or workplace and provide lifetime support of the life enhancing products that they purchase through the company.

The Disability Discrimination Act (DDA) 2005 and Equality Act 2010 means that employers have a legal requirement to ensure that they have appropriate technology and training available for those they employ that are blind, visual impaired or have learning, reading and writing difficulties. Sight and Sound Technology's solutions have changed the lives of those who use them. The company enables those with visual impairment to become employed whilst enabling employers to meet their equal opportunity and accessibility targets by undertaking bespoke development work on their corporate IT systems so that those with visual impairment are able to use them.

Sight and Sound Technology works in conjunction with its customers and suppliers to ensure that their experiences are factored into every new product that it develops in combination with its partners, the leading companies in the industry

The business began as a specialist business computer solutions provider, but it soon became interested in the technology that was developing for those with visual impairment. This was long before the miniaturised personal computers (PCs) that we have today. Computers then were called Main Frame computers and filled entire

Top: *Founder, Mervyn Robertson.* ***Left and above:*** *Early Main Frame computers.*

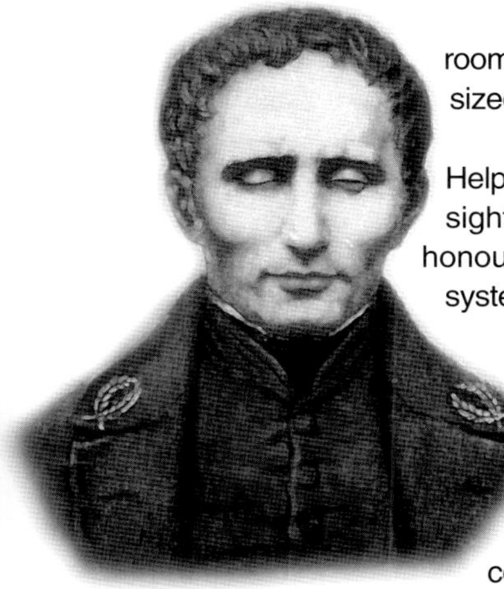

rooms, sometimes football pitch sized rooms!

Help for the blind and partially sighted has a long and honourable history. The Braille system, for example, of reading by touch, was based on a method of communication originally developed by Charles Barbier in response to the Emperor Napoleon's demand for a code that soldiers could use to communicate silently and without light at night – it was at first called 'night writing'. However, Barbier's system of sets of 12 embossed dots encoding 36 different sounds was too difficult for soldiers to perceive by touch, and it was rejected by the military. In 1821 Barbier visited the National Institute for the Blind, in Paris, where he met a blind man, Louis Braille. Braille identified the two key problems: first, by representing only sounds, the code was unable to give the orthography of the words; secondly, the human fingertip could not encompass the whole symbol without moving, and so could not move rapidly from one symbol to another. Braille's modification was to use a six dot cell - the Braille system - to represent each letter of the alphabet.

At first Braille's system was simply a one-to-one transliteration of French, but soon various Braille abbreviations and contractions were developed, creating a system much more

like shorthand - and the Braille system is still used today. Not until the advent of computers would Braille be challenged as the best and most convenient way for the blind and visually impaired to 'read' for themselves.

Sight and Sound Technology's co-founder was Mervyn Robertson. In 1979, with a partner, John Bradburn, he set up a commercial computer maintenance business with just four employees. The first premises were in a 'granny annexe' at 33, Harborough Road, Northampton.

At a local trade show at Durngate, Northampton, in 1980 Mervyn spoke to someone who had come across some 'interesting technology' in the USA which was being developed by a company called Maryland Computer Services, owned by Deane Blazie.

In 1981 Mervyn travelled to Baltimore in the USA and met with Deane Blazie and Ted Henter, who was also

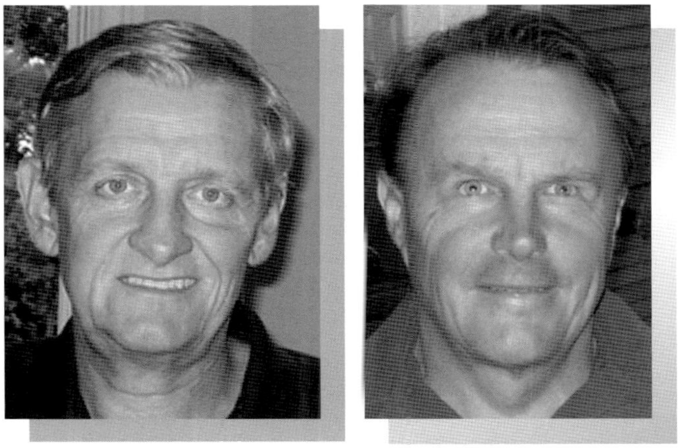

working with Maryland. Henter received some initial training in how to use a talking terminal from Deane Blazie and Maryland Computer Services, which later hired him to represent their products in the USA.

When he was 14 years old Deane Blazie went to a Ham radio club meeting where he met a blind man - Tim Cranmer - who at the time was Director of Services for the Blind in Kentucky. Blazie was fascinated with how much Cranmer was able to do despite being blind.

For the next few years Cranmer employed Blazie as his 'Saturday boy' doing odd jobs and helping him to build electronic devices. Cranmer would have ideas about solving a problem - like how does a blind person measure a voltage or current. Tim Cranmer invented a lot of little things for the blind, such as a device which when hung in a cup of coffee beeped when it was full.

Top left: *Louis Braille, inventor of the Braille reading and writing system for the blind and visually impaired. Braille himself was left blind after an accident as a small child.* ***Above left:*** *A refreshable Braille display.* ***Top right:*** *Deane Blazie (left) and Ted Henter.* ***Above and below:*** *Tim Cranmer, inventor of many instruments for the blind and visually impaired including the Cranmer abacus (below).*

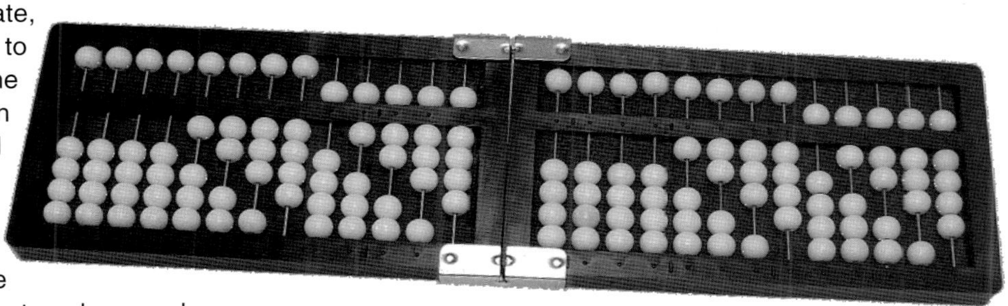

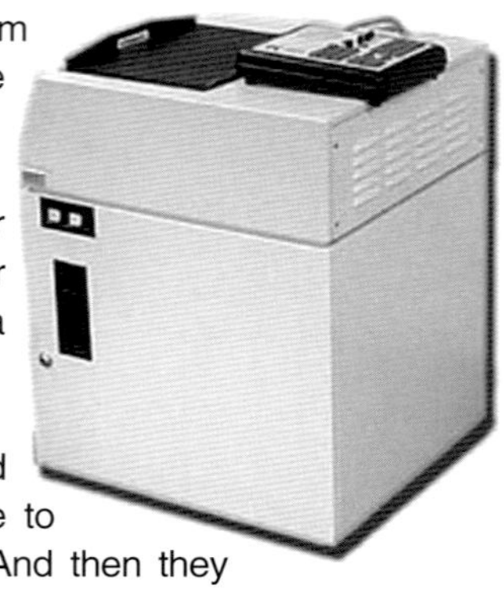

After Blazie left college Cranmer asked him to help develop a talking calculator for the blind.

Blazie founded Maryland Computer Services in 1976. A year later Tim Cranmer called him to ask if he could develop a speaking telephone directory.

That product led in turn to a word processing system enabling blind people to type and take notes and correct them. And then they added a full speech reader - a system which would speak any words which appeared on a computer screen.

When hooked up to a computer terminal, that device would eventually make it possible for people to get jobs as computer programmers, data entry clerks or in call centres - just about any kind of work that required using a computer.

The United States of America was where the leading edge development was being undertaken. Mervyn Robertson soon met the founding fathers of the entire industry – not least Ray Kurzweil. A serial entrepreneur, Ray had invented the Kurzweil Reading Machine. It was revolutionary – though it was the size of a washing machine and required a fork lift truck and a small van to transport it, one could feed a page of printed text into it and it would read it back. For the blind, it was the beginning of independence, mobility and access to information previously hidden from their sightless world. Today that reading machine is software on a pocket-sized mobile phone - how times have changed!

The blind and visually impaired side of the business in the USA was still relatively small compared to the core business of supplying and maintaining businesses computer systems.

In 1982, however, Sight and Sound Technology became the UK Exclusive/Master distributor for Information Through Speech (ITS) - at this time still attached to mainframe computers. It was soon to be followed by Total Talk PC as computing moved from HP 125 to personal computing.

Things were changing quickly. Sight and Sound Technology now moved to new premises at St James, Mill Road, Northampton.

That same year Kurzweil Computer Products and Ray Kurzweil approached Sight and Sound Technology to become UK exclusive distributor of its technology - KRM 400. As a consequence Sight and Sound Technology would eventually become more and more known as the expert in this field, and its Assistive Technology work would come to dominate the business.

The Kurzweil Personal Reader was launched in 1983. Three years later, however, Maryland Computer Services ceased trading. Deane Blazie set up Blazie Engineering; the new company would be instrumental in the development of other hardware products for the blind, including Braille embossers and refreshable Braille displays.

Left:** Ray Kurzweil demonstrating his first 'Kurzweil Reading Machine' to Kenneth Jernigan, President of the National Federation of the Blind USA in 1977.* ***Above right: *Ray Kurzweil, author, entrepreneur and inventor.* ***Top pictures:*** *The first model KRM (Kurzweil Reading Machine) circa 1978 (left), the KRM 400 of 1982 and a 1983 Kurzweil Personal Reader (bottom).*

In 1987 Kurzweil introduced 'The Reading Edge'. That same year Ted Henter teamed up with Bill Joyce to found Henter-Joyce and began development of the screen-reading software product for the blind, 'JAWS' (Job Access With Speech), originally a screen reader for Microsoft DOS, and later Windows 97.

Also in 1987, Ben Wise, the founder of AiSquared, Vermont, in the USA began developing a screen magnification software product for DOS. Sight and Sound Technology became the UK and Ireland Exclusive distributor for Aisqaured's product Zoom Text Screen Magnifier. Sight and Sound Technology continue to develop relationships with these key players in the Blind/Visually Impaired and Access technology market.

By 1989 Sight and Sound Technology had grown to have 65 employees and now built new premises - Qantel House, Moulton Park, Northampton. The building was formally opened by the Duke of Gloucester.

At the time it moved into Qantel House, Sight and Sound Technology had become the Master/Exclusive distributor for the world's leading screen reading, screen magnification and Braille products.

The products available would become ever more sophisticated as computer technology developed apace. In 1997 new scanning software, the Kurzweil 1000 for the Blind, and the Kurzweil 3000 for those with reading and writing difficulties, was launched.

As the computing revolution gained pace personal computers started to proliferate and customers began to demand technology that operated on a Windows platform.

Henter-Joyce merged with Blazie Engineering and Arkenstone in the year 2000 to form Freedom Scientific - the world's leading manufacturer of screen reading software, JAWS, and other accessible software and hardware equipment.

As the new millennium arrived Sight and Sound Technology entered the Education Market as an accredited supplier for Disabled Students Allowance (DSA) - supplying hardware, software, support and training to higher education students.

Above *In 1987 'The Reading Edge' was launched. Its unmatched speed and text recognition brought more time reading and less time waiting.* ***Below:*** *In 1997, with the arrival of personal computers, Kurzweil Education developed and marketed a new generation of educational software products.for persons with reading disabilities, ADHD, low vision, and visual impairment. Its two product lines were the Kurzweil 1000 and Kurzweil 3000, seen below at Landmark College.*

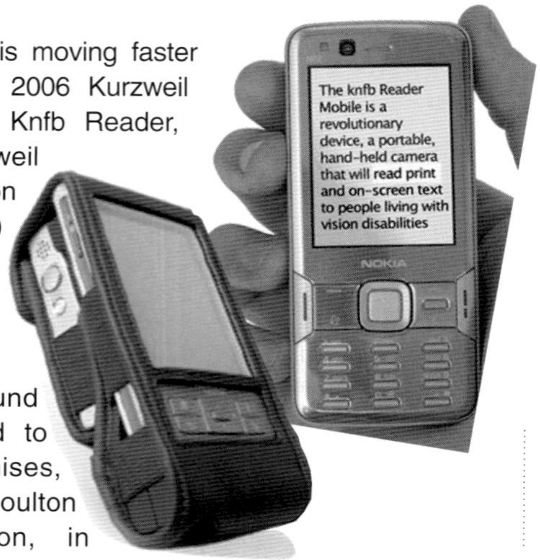

Mobile technology is moving faster and faster and in 2006 Kurzweil launched the first Knfb Reader, (short for Kurzweil National Federation of the Blind Reader) soon to be followed by the Knfb Reader MOBILE.

Sight and Sound Technology moved to its existing premises, Welton House, Moulton Park, Northampton, in 2008.

Today, Sight and Sound Technology is the leading player in a highly specialised market. The company looks after over 25,000 people with visual impairment and over 10,000 people with literacy support challenges. The world of technology moves ever faster and the company brings the newest innovations to people UK-wide, taking the time to make sure that they understand how to use the technology and how to contact the company when things go wrong - which as we all know with technology happens from time to time! Trained staff visit users in their home or workplace and provide lifetime support of the life-enhancing products that they purchase from the company.

With over 40 specialist partners and many corporate relationships, Sight and Sound Technology provides leadership and guidance to a wide range of groups.

Community involvement is an important part of the company ethos. Sight and Sound Technology has a long association with charities for the blind and visually impaired, supporting many good causes down the decades. In 2010 Sight and Sound Technology was the main sponsor for the English Blind Golf Association World Championships held at Whittlebury Park, Northampton. It was there that staff met with PC David Rathband. The firm supported David and the newly formed Blue Lamp Foundation in their quest to support all personnel of the police force, the fire service and the ambulance service who have been injured whilst on duty.

Glenn Tookey, the company's CEO, says "We are proud of our heritage and being at the centre of the assistive technology industry, and feel that it is fitting to be in the centre of the UK - Northampton.

"We are proud of our reputation over the past 30 years and more, as the leading supplier of equipment and services to the blind, visually impaired people and those with learning difficulties within the United Kingdom. Our professional standing is built upon our reputation for being large enough to supply and support market leading, high quality solutions, but small enough to listen to what our customers want and to care how we meet their needs.

Top left: *The 2006 and 2008 Kurzweil Knfb Readers.* ***Above:*** *In 2010 Sight and Sound Technology visited Support 4 Sight to advise and demonstrate their latest range of technology to assist visually impaired people.* ***Left:*** *In 2010 Sight and Sound Technology were proud to sponsor the Blue Lamp Foundation's 1st Annual Celebrity Golf Challenge and Gala Dinner.*

"Our aim is to bring the most technologically advanced equipment and software to the blind, visually impaired and those with learning difficulties at prices designed to match all budgets and to meet the diverse spectrum of individual needs – in education, the work place and at home.

"Emphasis is placed on putting the customer first by supplying quality at competitive prices. Equally important is the support offered by our highly trained service personnel."

It is almost 200 years since Braille was invented to help the blind and visually impaired. In the last three decades or so modern technology has come to offer a worthy successor to that wonderful invention. Today's computers would have seemed like magic to our predecessors. Without doubt the future services offered by Northampton's Sight and Sound Technology company will prove even more magical.

Left: *A selection of Sight and Sound Technology's products.* ***Below left:*** *Sight and Sound Technology's hand held magnifier - RUBY, a very popular product.* ***Below:*** *CEO, Glenn Tookey and founder, Mervyn Robertson.* ***Bottom:*** *The company's Welton House, Moulton Park, Northampton, premises.*

ROYAL VISITS

The Prince of Wales honoured the town with a visit on 7 July 1927. As the heir to the throne, Edward Albert Christian George Andrew Patrick David, to give him his full mouthful of a name, received a noisy and cheery welcome from the pupils of the High School for Girls. It was founded in 1878 by a church committee connected with Peterborough diocese. It was based on Derngate, before relocating in the early 1990s to a site on the Newport Pagnall road. Two baronesses, Marcia Falkender, former private secretary to Harold Wilson, and Eliza Manningham-Buller, once director of MI5, are old girls of the school. The future Edward VIII also paid a visit to the County Cricket Ground on Wantage Road to watch a physical training display put on by some other schoolchildren. This sporting venue was famous for also being the home of Northampton's professional soccer team, until it moved to Sixfields in 1994. The Prince of Wales had some sporting interests of his own. He was a useful lawn tennis player, though it was his brother, the future George VI, who played in the 1926 Wimbledon Championships. During the late 1920s and early 1930s, Edward was something of a celebrity, with his good looks and bachelor status. It was to all end in controversy in late 1936

when he abandoned the British throne in order to marry the American divorcée, Wallis Simpson. In the picture left the royal motorcade swept along Gold Street, past Grose's Garage. The town enjoyed visits from two future kings within the space of just a few years. The Prince of Wales, later to be Edward VIII, came in 1927 and his brother, the Duke of York, who would succeed him as George VI, was a welcome caller in May 1930, during festival week.

Three excellent images from the Royal visit in 1932 of the Duke and Duchess of York, later to become King George VI and Queen Elizabeth. They were in Northampton to open the new College of Technology and visit the John Greenwood Shipman Convalescent Home. The Duchess appears to be particularly relaxed in the photographs, whilst members of the official party seem rather more stiff and formal. The Duchess was seen to be radiating the charm for which she was to become famous. The official party included the Mayor and Mayoress, Councillor and Mrs P F Hanafy, Colonel John Brown and John Williamson, the Chief Constable. Huge crowds had gathered along the streets to get a view of the royal couple on their journey from Blisworth Station. In the main picture, we can see them alighting from the royal car outside the County Hall in George Row.

Above and right: Seen here leaving the nurses' home at the General Hospital, Princess Elizabeth made the short walk to the children's ward and the Barratt Maternity Home, accompanied by Earl Spencer. Having left the formality of the presentation behind, it was during this part of the visit that the happiest and most touching scenes of the day were enacted. The Princess met children whose ages ranged from five days to nine years, and children are nothing if not spontaneous. Outside the children's ward, in the warm sunshine, she chatted with 14 children surrounded by their toys. She was obviously moved, however, by the plight of some of the sick children. The Princess then went on to mingle with the mothers and expectant mothers in the Maternity Home. The home, was presented to Northampton by Mr W Barratt, the prominent shoe manufacturer. Hence, 'to walk the Barratt way' in Northampton, means to be pregnant. It is doubtful if anyone informed the Princess of this! Marking Princess Elizabeth's first official visit, 30 July, 1946, was a 'red letter' day for the town. In 1944 the hospital war appeal for £250,000 had been launched, with each town and village in the area allotted a target. The Princess was visiting the hospital to award souvenir

cards to the delegates of 103 places which had exceeded their target. The 7th Earl Spencer, was a British peer and the paternal grandfather of Diana Spencer, later to marry Prince Charles and become known as the much loved Princess Diana.

Bottom left: After the Japanese attack on Pearl Harbour in late 1941 brought America into the Second World War, it was not long before the USA had troops stationed in Europe as it broadened its commitment to the Allied cause. In February 1942, a small unit of the United States Army Air Force (USAAF) was set up in High Wycombe. By the end of the year, the Eighth USAAF was well established in bases across Britain. The wing of the 1st Air Division covered Northamptonshire and Cambridgeshire. The Americans used a number of local airfields that included RAF Grafton Underwood, designated USAAF 106 and RAF Kettering (Harrington), or USAAF 179, that was used later on in the war. They were also located at Chelveston, Deenethorpe, Polebrook, Spanhoe and Kings Cliffe. In July 1942, the first American B17 bombers and P38 fighters and crews arrived in Britain. Two years later, the Eighth Air Force had grown to become the biggest military air fleet ever seen. By this time, it had 122 bases, 200,000 personnel, 2,000 four engined bombers and 1,000 fighters. In 1946, Queen Elizabeth, wife of George VI, and her daughter, Princess Elizabeth, called at an American base during their visit to the county. This helped illustrate the debt that we owed to our allies from across the Atlantic and, in particular, to those who could never return to their homeland.

Right: Over in Market Square, at the offices of the 'Chronicle and Echo,' a more than life size portrait of the new Queen is being carefully put into position. The crowning of a young queen captured everybody's imagination and the atmosphere was full of new found optimism. The Coronation, in June 1953, was the first real national celebration since VE Day in 1945. Even that had been tinged by anxiety and sadness for some, and had been followed by continued years of shortages and rationing. This event marked a psychological moment in terms of letting go of the past and turning towards the future. The portrait on the front of the newspaper offices is so striking that Northamptonians who were living at the time will surely remember it. The whole of that unforgettable day will have impressed itself on the mind. The operation looks to be quite a tricky one and a health and safety nightmare, as workmen cling to ladders and hang out of windows.

Plans being put into place in Market Square on the morning of 9 July, 1965. Further examination of the photograph reveals soldiers, nurses and boy scouts. All these uniformed groups had been brought in by bus and van to play their part in what was to be a very happy occasion - the visit of Queen Elizabeth II and the Duke of Edinburgh to the town. The maroon Rolls Royce crossed the borough boundary at Weston Favell for the Queen's first visit to Northampton as a reigning monarch. Hundreds of flag-waving and cheering children made sure that she received a very special welcome. The crowds were extremely dense towards the town centre, some people having gained vantage points at top floor windows, or even on roof tops. 'Doesn't she look lovely,' was the cry as the Queen, in a lemon outfit, stepped out of the Rolls Royce at the Guildhall. Here the royal couple were entertained to lunch by the Mayor and Mayoress, Councillor and Mrs Don Wilson, before proceeding on their way, once more to great displays of enthusiasm. Local Northamptonians would no doubt have visited many of the businesses which can clearly be seen in the background. They include the Peal Assurance building, Lipton, advertising 'The Best Bacon', Milletts for jeans and slacks, the Queen's Arms and Scholl, promoting their brand of foot comfort service.

MILLETTS
A Phipps House
Scholl foot comfort service
MILLETTS
LET BY
Scholl

WARTIME

Below: The brave men of the Welsh Guards marched determinedly past F J Taylor's drapery store. Passing through Northampton on their way to the front in the early months of what was to become known initially as the Great War, the streets were lined with well wishers cheering them on. Many thought that this was going to be a great adventure and a good way in which to impress the girls who just loved a man in uniform. With thoughts that it would all be over by Christmas, the soldiers and their loved ones were in for a rude awakening. There was not even a period of a 'phoney war' such as the one experienced in the first few months of the 1939-45 conflict. Here, war was declared in early August 1914 and the British Expeditionary Force of about 70,000 men crosses the Channel. Yet, within a few, short weeks they were retreating from Mons, having suffered heavy casualties.

Above: Councillor Henry Butterfield JP rose to the lofty office of Mayor of Northampton in 1909. He was still a redoubtable figure on the local scene a decade later. These girls were pleased, or at least one of them seemed to be, to have their fellow pupils' work for the war effort acknowledged by this handsome plaque. They were students at Campbell Square School who took part in the National Egg Collecting drive, under the patronage of Queen Alexandra, Edward VII's widow. Children were encouraged to 'do their bit' and help provide nourishment for wounded soldiers recuperating from injuries received fighting the foe during World War I. The eggs were sent to one of the 2,000 depots eventually established up and down the country. At the start of the war, some 12,000 were collected on a weekly basis. This rose to 150,000 by the end of 1916, but the director of operations pleaded for still more, saying that even a million per week would not be enough. The children of Campbell Square School were the best gatherers in the whole of the borough and well deserved their plaque and the gratitude of those whose recovery had been helped by their efforts.

Did you know?

During the Civil War (1642 – 1651) Northampton shoemakers supplied the Parliamentary armies with 600 pairs of boots and 4,000 pairs of shoes. And during both world wars supplied most of the boots worn by the British armed forces.

Above: This octet of beauties showed that you could have looks as well as brains. They were members of a special demonstration platoon of the War Office who were given the task of showing others how to perform tasks that varied from the mundane to the skilful and dangerous. Some Auxiliary Territorial Service (ATS) women arranged field cooking sessions or lorry driving lessons, while others demonstrated the stripping down of guns and the safe handling of explosives. Women had served in the First World War, but their branch of the Army had been disbanded in 1921. Various volunteer groups carried on, but no official body existed until the mid 1930s when the Women's Emergency Service was formed. This developed into the new ATS body in September 1938. Initially, the women's roles were confined to those that they traditionally held in civvy street, but as more and more men were called up after war had been declared the gender barriers were breached. ATS duties soon included radar operators, military police, anti-aircraft gun command posts and many other operational support tasks. By the end of hostilities there were over 190,000 ATS members. The women seen here were taking a short break on their way back from RAF Brackley, later known as RAF Croughton, that had a particular wartime role as a training facility. The group was probably heading back to the Racecourse where many ATS personnel were billeted.

Left: Northampton can count itself lucky. It suffered little from the bombing raids of the Luftwaffe during World War II. Try telling that to the owners of the bungalows near Bants Lane. Their homes disintegrated. The tin hat hanging from the bicycle was little protection against the stick of bombs that created such havoc. Northampton's first experience of the mayhem came in August 1940 across Duston and St James' End. Although only 38 bombs landed on the town, one was enough if you were underneath it. Those hit in the raids lost their homes and prized possessions. They had to start all over again.

Above: Even in 1944 normal life continued. Buses trundled up the street and women indulged in window shopping. Clothing was rationed. Material was needed for uniforms, army greatcoats and parachutes. Mums got out the sewing machine and turned curtains into frocks. Petrol was restricted to essential use and cars were put into mothballs until the end of the war. As best we could, we tried to carry on with our normal routines. However, the shelter on the Drapery reminded us that, however hard we tried to forget, there was still a war on. At first sight this one looks like a Tardis, that miraculous time travel contraption that was a hundred times larger inside than out. The shelter could take 70 people, according to the sign on top. Where would they all fit? The answer is boringly simple. A labyrinth of old cellars and vaults ran under the town centre. This box covered just one of the entrances. Similar structures were dotted all around the centre, giving speedy access to underground safety in case of an emergency. The stories that people told after their time beneath the Drapery pavement gave rise to legends about secret tunnels. Fanciful storytellers conjured up images of hooded monks, secret lovers and smugglers making their way along the winding passages.

Did you know?

The first Battle of Northampton took place at the site of Northampton Castle in 1264 when the forces of Henry III overran the supporters of Simon de Montfort, 6th Earl of Leicester.

In 1460, a second Battle of Northampton took place in the grounds of Delapré Abbey and was a decisive battle of the 'Wars of the Roses'. King Henry VI was captured in the town by the House of York.

Right: As a nation we were slow to accept the threat to our freedom that, with hindsight, seems all too obvious now. Having won one great war, it seemed unlikely that the vanquished power could rise again so swiftly and so ferociously to be in a position to threaten our shores within a couple of decades. But, it happened, and after the German invasion of Czechoslovakia, in late 1938, it meant we had to get ready for modern warfare, and quickly. Civil defence groups were formed and air raid precautions made a priority. We had seen what dive bombers could do to Guernica, so we dug underground shelters, like these being constructed on the Racecourse. Householders built their own in their gardens or took advantage of the free or cut price Anderson shelters on offer from the government. Cellars in large buildings and subterranean areas on the London Underground were also earmarked for use. People practised for the real thing, but nothing really prepared them for the noise, fear and sheer devastation that came for real during the Blitz of 1940-41.

Everybody did his bit for the war effort. Those in uniform served in the armed forces either at home or overseas. Others took on roles in reserved occupations or volunteered for various positions within civil defence organisations. We dug for victory, made do and mended, collected scrap and salvage, bought war bonds and gave generously to a number of fund raising activities. During the early 1940s there were special drives for contributions that were linked to a particular theme. This helped focus people's attention, rather than just holding out the begging bowl. Each year seemed to bring its own very special campaign. In 1940, it was the Spitfire Fund, followed by War Weapons Week in the next year. In 1942, we had Warship Week, with Wings for Victory 12 months later. Salute the Soldier Week came to Northampton in May 1944, the month before D-Day, though we did not know it. Children clambered over tanks as if they were playthings, though the grown-ups knew the value and true purpose of these machines. These campaigns were supported by everyone and succeeded in uniting civilians and service personnel in the common aim of winning the war. In October 1945, a Spitfire was brought into Market Square as part of the celebrations in Thanksgiving Week, held to mark our gratitude to those who had brought us through the dark hours and helped release the bluebirds over the white cliffs once more.

Above: It was all very well for women to move into the factories during World War II and take over the jobs that the men at the front had left vacant. Although they could happily fill those shoes, they still had another vital role to play, namely the traditional one of home maker and mother. Whilst they were filling cartridges, packing parachutes, turning lathes or driving lorries someone had to care for the children who were too young to go to school. The solution was straightforward. Companies and councils provided crèches so that the kiddies could be watched over and cared for in safety while their mums did their bit for the war effort. Sometimes, it was the souls of the children as well as their bodies that received care and attention. Saying grace before a meal was quite a common practice in schools, so it was no surprise to find that these little ones at the Dallington crèche were encouraged to thank their maker for all that was bountiful on their plates. The prayers did not last long when Woolton pie, that unpopular mix of diced vegetables topped by pastry, was on the menu.

Below: These hordes of excited wartime children are not digging for victory, but are searching for shrapnel. The occasion was in October 1940 when a returning German bomber jettisoned its remaining bomb on a field in Weston Favell. Northampton got off very lightly in terms of bombing during World War II, compared with nearby Coventry. Nevertheless, two incidents occurred which, but for good fortune, could have caused heavy casualties. In January 1941 bombs demolished buildings at St Andrew's Hospital and left huge craters in Billing Road Cemetery. Tombstones crashed through neighbouring roofs, unbelievably without any loss of life. Ironically, however, the worst damage of all was done by a British plane, later in the war. A crippled Stirling bomber, abandoned by its crew at night over open land, changed course of its own accord. The empty plane roared dramatically down Gold Street and crashed in George Row. It was a miracle that know one was hurt as the planes wing tips apparently scored a mark down buildings on either side of the street.

EVENTS & OCCASIONS

The Northamptonshire Regiment was formed in 1881 by the amalgamation of the 48th Regiment of Foot and the 58th (Rutlandshire) Regiment of Foot. These units had been originally raised in 1741 and 1755, respectively. They saw active service on many fronts, particularly during the Napoleonic Wars. After coming together as one regiment, the two battalions fought nobly in the Boer War, as well as doing service in Hong Kong,

Singapore and India. The field behind the Drill Hall on Clare Street provided an open space where practice routines and ceremonial procedures could be carried out. The men of the 1/4th Battalion cut handsome figures as they stood to attention on an occasion during the first decade of the 20th century. Most of these men would be marching off to war once more in a few years' time. The 1914-18 War saw the regiment expand to comprise 13 battalions, most of whom served on the western front in France and Flanders, as well as contributing to the campaigns at Gallipoli, in Egypt and in Palestine. The regiment was reduced to a single battalion in 1948 and became part of the 2nd East Anglian Regiment in 1960, which in turn morphed into the Royal Anglian Regiment in 1964. The drill field is now covered over by a housing development known as Military Court. However, the old army barracks on Clare Street is still in use as a Territorial Army centre. Soldiers undertake some evening and weekend, military and physical training.

Below: The crowds gathered in Regent Square on 22 June, 1897, to celebrate the 60th anniversary of Queen Victoria's accession to the throne. No other British monarch had made it to a diamond jubilee, though her grandfather King George III was only just over 250 days short of achieving that milestone. Regent Square took its name from the title given to Victoria's uncle, the future George IV, when he acted in the place of his father during that king's 'madness'. The fountain seen here was erected in 1860, having been paid for by public subscription. It was dedicated to the memory of the Reverend Thomas Hutton, a former chaplain of the County Gaol. He served in that capacity for 11 years and was also remembered for his sterling work in support of temperance and education for the masses. Unfortunately, the monument was badly damaged when a car crashed into it in December 1953. It is not known whether the driver was as sober as the Reverend Hutton would have wished. Sadly, all trace of the fountain was cleared away and never brought back to life.

Did you know?

St Crispin is the patron saint of shoemakers. Since medieval times 25 October has been celebrated as St. Crispin's Day and the Shoemaker's Holiday. In the past, boot and shoemakers traditionally closed their shops on this day in celebration and commemoration.

Above: We did not get a National Health Service until after the last war. Before then, the country relied on a mixture of subscription, charitable provision, private funding, local authority support and benevolence to fund its medical services. The cycle parade in the foreground, with riders acting as clowns and musicians, was just part of a larger ensemble who gathered here on an annual basis. They joined with other groups and organisations on a march through town as they urged those watching in the crowd to give generously. This Market Square scene took place on 17 July, 1911, and was the 21st of its type, the forerunner of the Carnival Parades of later years. Contributions went towards the running of the General Hospital, an establishment that was always in need of funds. Since people never knew when they might have to call on its nursing services, they gave generously. Northampton General Hospital first opened in 1743. It was known as the County Infirmary and sited at George Row. In 1793, it changed to the General Infirmary when the new hospital was built in Billing Road. During this early period, it served as a voluntary hospital. In 1903, it again changed its title to the present Northampton General Hospital. The Carnival became established as such after the 1914-18 War and continued to be a source of much merriment and enjoyment for most of the remainder of the century. A break with tradition occurred in the late 1990s, but the Carnival was happily restored in 2005.

PHŒNIX
J. SAINSBURY
ASSURANC
James

In the scene centred upon the gathering around the former fountain, the distinctive art deco newspaper offices in the background on the right were demolished in 1978 to make way for the expansion of the Grosvenor Centre. Further over to the right a First Choice travel shop is now based in Welsh House. This was built in 1595 and was one of the few buildings to survive the Great Fire. It gets its name from the Welsh heritage of its owner, Dr Prytherch. The façade was rebuilt in 1975. The gathered crowd was listening to the proclamation announcing the succession of Queen Elizabeth II on the occasion of the death of her father in 1952. The new monarch was on her way back from a holiday in Kenya at the time. In the accompanying image, locals gathered in Market Square to celebrate her coronation in June the following year. The buildings on the far side of the square now include Barclays instead of Sainsbury's, with a photo and digital specialist to the right of the bank and William Hill's beyond that.

Did you know?

78 Derngate is a Grade II listed Georgian Town House remodelled by Charles Rennie Mackintosh for Wenman Joseph Bassett-Lowke in 1916–17. It contains notable Mackintosh interiors (which have been restored) and is his only major domestic commission outside Scotland.*

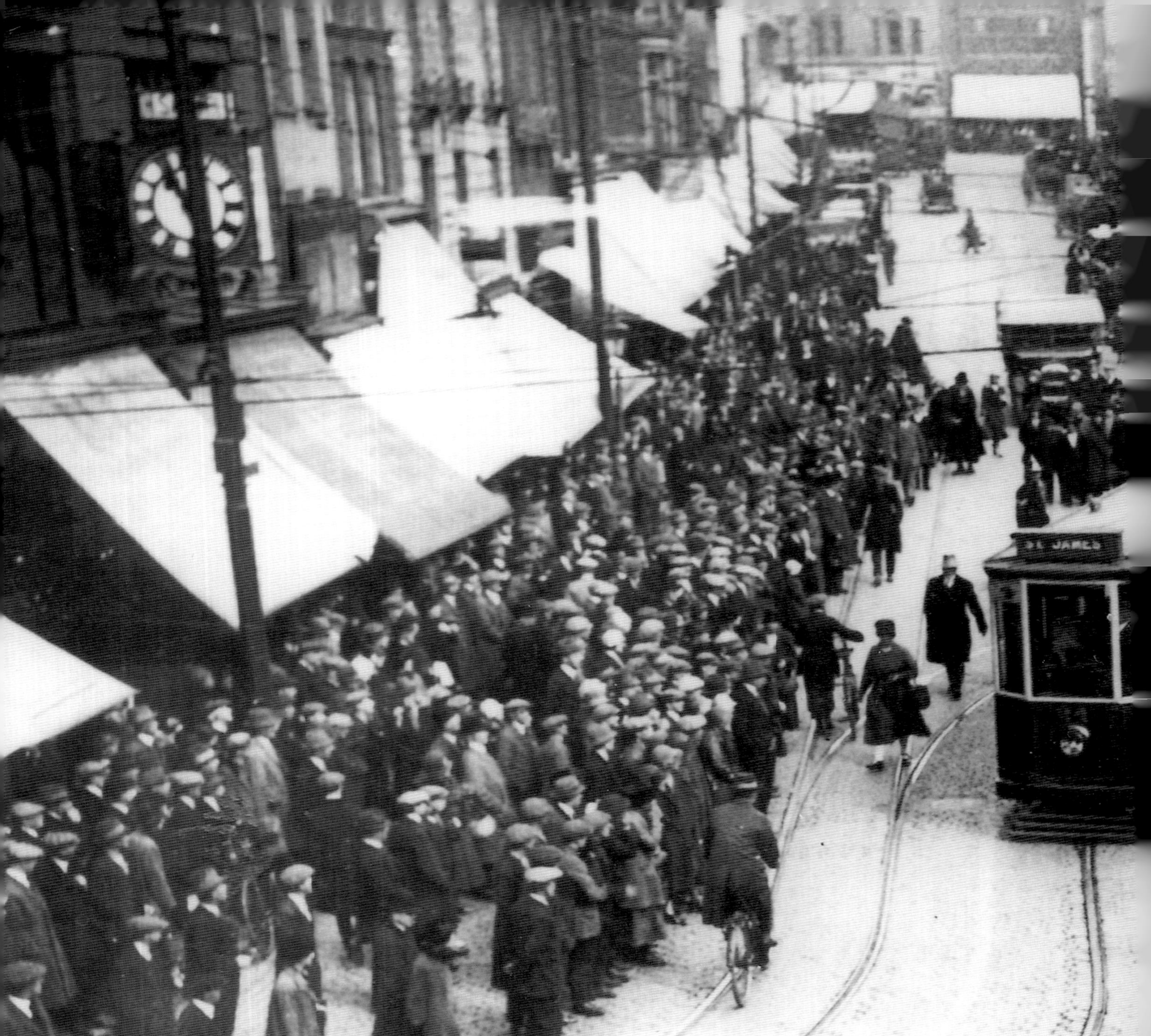

Lloyd George and his government promised 'homes fit for heroes' when the First World War came to an end. Foolishly, the rank and file believed him. They should have known better, having experienced the horrors of the European ridges and trenches and the assault beaches of Gallipoli and other awful places. Since generals and their like showed scant regard for the common man, how was it that the population accepted the words of politicians? They were soon to find out the truth. The country had huge war debts and the world was heading for recession. Investment in industry had been scant and the 1920s offered little in the way of hope for the future. Jobs were hard to find, living conditions poor and wages were kept as low as possible by those holding the purse strings. Winston Churchill oversaw the reintroduction of the gold standard, effectively making the British pound too strong for successful exporting of manufactured goods. When mine owners tried to introduce wage cuts to offset a reduction in productivity, the workforce rebelled. Other workers joined in the protests and a General Strike was called in May 1926. On the corner of The Drapery and Mercer's Row, a crowd of strikers demonstrated against the running of the Corporation trams. The tramways manager, Mr Cameron, thought that he could break the strike by taking the controls of a tram himself. He was nearly lynched by an angry crowd who also tried to drag passengers from the car. The police used batons as they charged the crowd and arrested the ringleaders. Many thought that Mr Cameron should have been arrested for incitement, but his part in the incident was ignored by the constabulary.

Above: We may not have had much, but we knew how to celebrate. Working class residents of terraced housing had little to spare and were experiencing the effects of the global recession that was known in the 1930s as the Great Depression. Unemployment was high and families struggled to find enough food to put on the table to keep body and soul together. Yet, along came a day of national rejoicing and they all joined in. Flags were flown and bunting spread across the street from one side to another. Mums searched their larders for whatever they could find to lay on a spread, mainly for the children. Tables were dragged out into the street and benches commandeered from schools and church halls. This was the day in May 1935 when the country marked the occasion of George V's silver jubilee. Up and down the nation the day was marked by celebrations, the like of which had not been seen since Armistice Day in late 1918.

Did you know?

Nothampton was home to a Nobel Prize winner - Weston Favell-born scientist Francis Crick, who with James D. Watson, discovered the structure of DNA. He won the award in 1962.

Right: A fabulously patriotic scene from 12 May, 1937, marking the Coronation of King George VI and Queen Elizabeth. In common with the rest of the country, Northampton celebrated the occasion with rejoicing and fervour. People were glad of a joyous royal event which might relieve the general gloom of national and international affairs at that time. Only the year before, in 1936, the abdication crisis concerning King Edward VIII's association with the American divorcee, Mrs Wallis Simpson, had caused constitutional problems. Northampton streets were lavishly decorated for the great day and this photograph shows The Drapery, looking down towards George Row. Shops and public buildings are hung with giant flags, and streamers criss-cross the street. Apart from the vehicles, the ladies' cloche hats on view give the scene a 1930s feel, as does the old lamp standard in the middle of the road. A shopper looking at the same scene now would probably be focusing on Debenhams, half-way down the right-hand side, where in 1937, Adnitt's store stood. The building immediately on the right of shot was the original Northamptonshire Union Bank; today it would be the Natwest.

Right: "You wait all day for a bus, then two come along at the same time," or as is the case in this scene, nine or ten at once. In fact, the queue of buses in Market Square was part of a Holidays at Home promotion by the Corporation Transport Department in the immediate post-war years. People had not been encouraged to travel during the Second World War, as petrol was in short supply and economy was the order of the day. This was encapsulated in the government slogan, 'Is Your Journey Really Necessary'? Things did not improve greatly even when the war was over and hence the 'Holidays at Home' campaign. During Northampton's annual summer shoe holiday fortnight, those who still could not get away could at least enjoy entertainments put on by the Corporation. One of the diversions was a bus tour of the suburbs which were in the process of being developed in the years after 1945. Apart from the line of buses in Market Square, an interesting array of old cars offers an identification challenge to automobile buffs. In the background the distinctive white facade of Burtons can be seen behind the buses, with Waterloo House to the far right and the well known, Roses Fashion Centre.

Right: Carnival time was popular with everyone. In 1937 thousands lined the streets to watch the parade of floats making their way up Gold Street into George Row. It came as a welcome distraction from the worrying news from Europe. The storm clouds of war were gathering. At home we could escape by looking at the pretty girls in their costumes. They flanked the contraptions that had been gaily decked with garlands and bunting to set off the festive scene. Later there would be games and sports in the parks. The fairground would be alive with the noise of happy folk enjoying the dodgems, coconut shies and merry go rounds. In the meantime the crowd thrilled at the ingenuity of the float designers. The main one pictured was called 'Showboat'. It was an entry by the Rushden shoe company of John White Ltd. Not surprisingly, it won the championship cup. Northampton's carnival had a long history. It began in 1890 as a cycle parade. At the time there were 12 cycling clubs in the town. The carnival raised funds for the General Hospital.

Bottom left: When the much awaited day of 2 June, 1953, at last arrived, the British weather naturally rose to the occasion. It was generally dull and cold, with squally bursts of rain. Nevertheless, the people of Northampton were determined to enjoy themselves and the weather did not prevent an eruption of street parties which had been planned for months. The photographer has caught an absolute sea of colour along Gladstone Terrace in a scene that was so typical of the day. Most of the celebrations took place in the afternoon as everyone wanted to watch the Coronation ceremony on television around midday. In 1953, of course, televisions were quite a rarity and there was a good deal of communal viewing of televisions set up in school and church halls. The screens were small and the images were black-and-white and of poor quality, but anyone who watched that day will not have forgotten the experience. Then it was off to the street parties! The children of Gladstone Terrace are obviously enjoying themselves. There are plenty of caps and short pants in evidence, for there was no pressure for children to look 'cool'. Gladstone Terrace ran off Barrack Lane and Adelaide Street, up near to the Racecourse.

Below: There are times when we wish that we could turn back the clock. Such an occasion can be seen here. On 15 April 1962, the fountain that had stood in Market Square for 99 years was dismantled. It was not even allowed an extra year of life so that it could reach its centenary. Erected in 1863, it had been raised by Samuel Isaacs, a local shoe manufacturer, to mark the the marriage of Prince Albert to Princess Alexandra of Denmark. He had been created the Prince of Wales in 1841 when just a month old. 'Bertie', as he was known, would eventually take the throne as Edward VII in 1901. The fountain was often used as a meeting point and also acted as a backdrop for speakers addressing crowds in the square. The council decided it had become unsafe and instructed its workmen to take it down, much to the disgust of many locals. No attempt was made at restoration and the fine monument became just so much scrap metal and stone. The steps were left in place and used for a while by market traders as somewhere to stack boxes and crates. It was an ignominious end.

TRANSPORT

Below: Plastered with adverts for whisky, baking powder and cocoa, the last of the town's horse drawn trams made its way to the Phippsville terminus, near St Matthew's Church. It was 1904 and the electrical age had arrived. The face of public transport would soon change, as would the illumination on our streets and the power sources within our

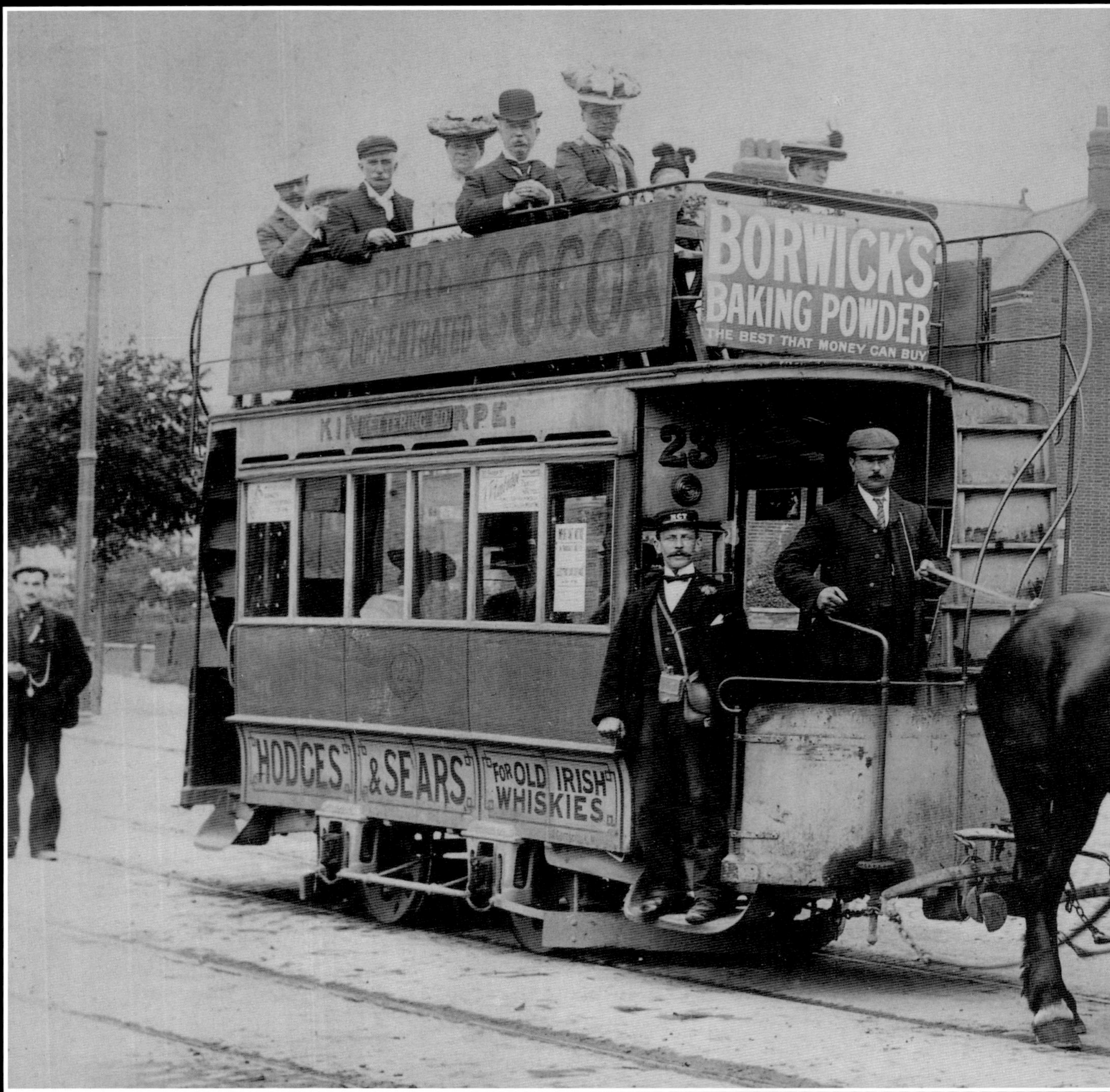

homes. Trams were first pulled by horses in Northampton in 1881. The first cars were single decker units operated by the Northampton Street Tramways Company. It was based in Abington Street where the Central Library now stands. The conductor, E Patrick, and driver, W Hawkins, had already undergone a period of training to help them transfer to the new electric trams and they were soon to be seen operating the new technology.

Above: The transport car belonging to the borough's special constabulary had been paid for by public subscription. Locals dipped into their pockets on one of the many occasions they would do so in order to give something towards the war effort. Seen in c1917, when the Great War was at its height, this vehicle was mainly used to take servicemen back on leave. We could not begrudge a few comforts to those who had faced the horrors of the trenches on the Somme or the ridge at Passchendaele. The special constabulary was, as it is today, a volunteer wing of the police force staffed by part time officers. In 1673, King Charles II decreed that ordinary citizens could be sworn in as temporary, emergency peace keepers in times of civil disorder. They were used more frequently during periods of protest against Parliament when calls for social reform in the early 19th century were loudly heard. The Special Constabulary was defined as a volunteer organisation, but with expanded powers, in an Act of 1835. At the start of the 1914-18 War, special constables were given the job of safeguarding water supplies from German infiltrators. Their remit was soon broadened when more and more regular policemen joined the armed forces and 'the specials' took on most of the duties undertaken by the regular police.

Did you know?

That the first car chase in Britain involving the police occurred in Northampton in 1899? Sergeant Hector Macleod got his man with screaming tyres – well, maybe tyres that were grumbling a bit.

Right: Crowds line the streets of Northampton to watch the official opening ceremony as the first electric tram leaves Mercer's Row on 21 July, 1904. By 1904, four main tram routes had been electrified and the St James depot was also built at that time. In this picture tramcars decorated with flowers and bunting set off with the Mayor and official party on board for the 10-minute journey to the St Matthew's Church tramway terminus. This was followed by a journey to the Franklin Gardens terminus and from there on to Abington Park. A fifth route out to Far Cotton was opened in 1914.

Left: The Kingsley Park Hotel had been standing for well over 20 years when the St James' tram trundled by. However, its prosperity was threatened at about this time because of the closure of the Racecourse in 1904. The Jockey Club took this decision after a number of spectators were killed in an accident at the course. Unfortunately, the decision severely damaged the hotel's trade. The Racecourse had previously been used during the 18th century, on occasions, as a place of public execution. It was not possible to resurrect such a recreational activity for the general public, so business at the Kingsley Park suffered! It became the White Elephant on an official basis in the 1950s and, with a brief change to being the Kingsley Park Tavern, has been that ever since.

Above: Joseph Grose was a pioneering cyclist. Among the feats that he achieved was topping 20 mph at the Leicester Cycle Track in July 1883 while riding a 52-inch-wheeled contraption. A keen supporter of penny farthing cycling, he opened a cycle shop in Horseshoe Street in the 1880s. Later moving premises to the corner with Gold Street, Grose discovered the joys of motorised travel. His first car was a three-wheeled model that was driven from a position above the engine, with his passenger comfortably seated in front of him. A new garage and revamped premises were opened on a 300 feet length of Pike Lane in 1912. The business continued to prosper and the workforce grew. Here we can see a number of employees from the 1920s waiting to go on a staff outing laid on by the company. Initially, Grose developed his company as a firm of coachbuilders. He concentrated on bespoke manufacture before branching out into developing some of his models into racing cars. The business gradually concentrated more on car dealership as the years passed and today, as W Grose Limited, is based on a five acre site at Kingsthorpe selling and servicing General Motors vehicles.

Above: Pictured in the years leading up to World War I, two types of tram from the Northampton Corporation Tramways Company made their way through the town centre. The leading car was headed for Abington Park while the open-topped one made its way to Kingsley. The first part of our electric tram route was opened on 21 July, 1904. Large crowds, numbering several thousand, packed the streets to witness the birth of this revolutionary form of public transport. The tram was not new as, in 1881, a horse drawn service was established from All Saints Church to the Kingsley Park Hotel, at the corner with St Matthew's Parade and the Racecourse. It was the modernity of the electric motor and its allied cabling that attracted men in their straw boaters and ladies under parasols to the Drapery and Mercer's Row as the first of the new era of public transport vehicles made its bow and glided along the track. The dominance of the electric tram only lasted for about a quarter of a century. The Corporation introduced buses in the 1920s and, by 1934, they had taken over completely. An old tram shelter can still be seen opposite the White Elephant. A second one has been preserved at the corner of Kingsthorpe Grove and Harborough Road, and very handsome they look, too.

Below and top right: The story of motorbuses in Northampton begins in 1928 when two six-wheeled Guy double-deckers were ordered to supplement trams on Wellingborough Road services. Trams were replaced next on the Kettering Road in 1930, whilst the last tram to Kingsthorpe ran on 27 September, 1933. Pictured right is a fine illustration of a Northampton Corporation 54-seater. This bus had a Grose built body on a 1931 Guy chassis. So successful were they, that this ultimately sealed the fete of the tramways system in Northampton. By the end of 1934, motorbuses reigned supreme. As the town and bus routes

expanded, an extension to the workshop and garage facilities at St James was opened.

Below: This was definitely the wrong sort of snow. The railways have come up with a variety of excuses for delays and disruptions to add to the famous one about leaves on the line, but the winter of 1962-63 contained some of the worst weather and the best of reasons as to why things ground to a halt. These workmen had just enjoyed a white Christmas only two days earlier, but now was the time to face reality. The line near Kingsthorpe Mill had become blocked and it was their task to clear a path for the locomotive and its carriages to continue on their journey. Easier said than done, as there were tons of the white stuff that had been blown into drifts by the biting wind that chilled the men to the marrow. This winter became known as the Big Freeze and the country was paralysed for weeks on end. Blizzards swept the country and, as New Year came in, temperatures as low as 16°C were recorded. The sea froze at Herne Bay and parts of the River Thames were iced over. Freezing fog added to the misery and sports fixtures were badly affected. The snow lay on the ground until early March. Ironically, by the middle of that month Cliff Richard was topping the hit parade with 'Summer Holiday'.

Did you know?

The first railway to be built into Northampton was a branch from the main London and Birmingham Railway Blisworth to Peterborough through Northampton which opened in 1845.

AT WORK

Below: Back in the early 1900s there was no such thing as the welfare state. If you fell on hard times, then charity was hard to come by, but all upon which you could rely. For those who suffered an affliction or disability, then life was tougher still. Blind Bellamy and Boy Joe were well known on our streets in Edwardian times. They were a cut above the beggars who hung around street corners, though they still had the obligatory dog with them as an attempt to tug at the heart strings. This pair, at least, offered something in the way of entertainment. They operated a barrel organ and hoped that those off to market or the local shops would open their purses and find the odd halfpenny that they could spare. The original barrel organ was a table top hand cranked affair used by ladies of leisure in the 18th century for their own personal entertainment. Larger versions were adopted by wandering troubadours and entertainers who deepened the shrill sound by adding larger pipes, bellows and interchangeable barrels. Some organ grinders, as they became known, used tame monkeys to collect coins from audiences. Some Victorian organs made music employing technology learned from the Jacquard looms used in the textile industry, whereby holes punched in rolls of card were 'read' by a machine. Others made use of pins and staples attached to the barrel that were 'played' by a set of levers.

Right: Present day members of the local health and safety brigade would rub their hands with glee at the scene outside this game dealer and fishmonger in the 1920s. This was a common sight at one time and no-one turned a hair (or should that be hare?) at the sight of poultry and game being hung out in the open. More to the point, nobody collapsed with stomach cramps after eating the meat, so what is so different about modern digestive systems? The magnificent display frame was constructed specially for the shop and H E Wilson, on the left, the owner's brother-in-law, used a carefully preserved long pole to access the turkeys and other creatures on the uppermost perches. Established in 1836 by John Clark at 2 George Row, between the entrance to the George Hotel mews and the Coach and Horses, the business passed to a Mr Brown before being taken over by F H Phillips. He helped boost the trade to such a degree that this outlet pictured at 17 Bridge Street was soon added. The firm also had a fish merchant's business on Tyneside and owned two steam powered fishing boats. Phillips adopted the telegraphic address 'Goldfish, Northampton', something of a forerunner to the personalised internet sites and emails of today. From roe to rabbit and from dab to duck, Phillips could supply it at the shops or via a home delivery service.

Did you know?

In the early 19th century more than a third of men worked in the shoe industry. In the late 19th century it rose to nearly half.

Margaret Bondfield, Labour MP for Northampton in 1923, was the first woman Cabinet minister in the United Kingdom and one of the first three female Labour MPs.

Stop here and Inspect our Stock
Best Quality

At 3.21pm workers are seen here taking a well deserved break and posing for the camera. They are working on laying the electric tramlines in Abington Square in 1904. The initial installation of the complete electric system cost £85,000. Power was supplied by burning the town's refuse in special boilers. During construction, 60 navvies working on the track went on strike for a 1d an hour rise, to increase their wages from 5 and

a half pence to 6 and a half pence an hour. The demand was refused. In the background is the People's Cafe and the statue of Charles Bradlaugh, MP for Northampton and a radical leader and campaigner for social and political justice. The café was later to suffer a serious fire. After repairs it became a leather mercer's warehouse and billiard hall. It was eventually demolished in 1933 and this view of the Square, is much different today.

Above: Brooklands Aviation was a busy centre during the last war. Its repair shop, here containing Wellington bombers, worked hard in turning jobs round, knowing that its role was vital in the war effort. Based at Sywell Aerodrome, the company used vast hangars in which planes were stripped to their frames and the fabric replaced. Workers had to hand sew the seams, using a regulation eight stitches to the inch. It was tiring and painstaking, but rewarding knowing that the finished product would soon be back in the air and attacking the enemy.

Facing page: Looking back at the archives, we can see that shoemaking was established in the town in early Tudor times when about one in seven was earning a living in this way. Even though everybody seems to associate the footwear trade with Northampton, it was not really until the 17th century that it took on significant commercial proportions, ousting wool as a major source of trade and industry. By the time the industrial revolution was fully under way, Northampton revelled in the label of 'tanning capital' of not just the country, but the world. Before then, much of the work was done at home in cottage industries. The arrival on the scene of the industrial sewing machine gave rise to a paired development that took the form of purpose-built small factories operating alongside specially erected premises next to the homes of 'outworkers'. Both the factories and workshops used women, in the main. Although some men, particularly in the smaller establishments, were deployed to work on the machines, it was their wives, mothers and daughters who generally operated the treadles. In the warehouse we can see row after row of hides in store, waiting to be treated and processed, eventually making it to the finishing rooms before being despatched for sale. The staff pictured on the factory floor look to be enjoying some form of royal celebration, if the bunting, Union flags and little crown headdresses are anything to go by. Some of the old factories have been converted into flats or offices and just a small handful, or should that be shoeful, of specialist firms continue in business today.

Did you know?

Boot and shoemakers are often commonly called 'cobblers'. But the word cobbler is more properly applied to shoe repairmen. Those who actually make footwear are known as 'cordwainers'. This term has its antecedents in the word 'cordovan' which was a reddish leather produced in Spain.

The Grosvenor Shopping Centre

The Most Modern of Shopping Experiences

Whether or not the ancient inhabitants of Northampton believed in the philosophy of 'shop till you drop' is a moot point - but it's a fair bet that they did. If the present is any guide to the past it's not hard to imagine our forebears centuries ago enjoying the town's commercial opportunities to the full.

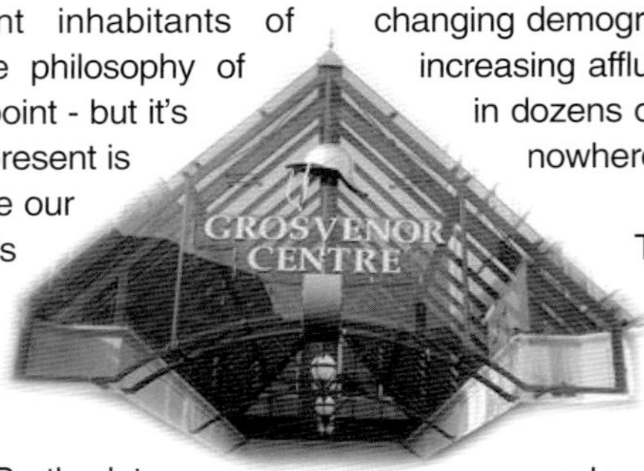

Throughout the length and breadth of England fairs, markets and temporary stalls eventually evolved into permanent shops. By the late 1950s, however, many of Britain's once thriving Victorian shopping centres were worn out and dated. Some had been badly damaged during the war. Neglect and deterioration, changing demographics and changing expectations along with increasing affluence was leading to calls for redevelopment in dozens of towns and cities all across the country. And nowhere more so than in Northampton.

The 'Swinging Sixties' was a decade of enormous optimism. Prime Minister Harold Wilson had promised to harness the 'white hot heat of technology' to further a new era of affluence and modernity. The world and our towns were changing before our very eyes. Through the music of the Beatles and the clothes designs of May Quant, Britain was at the vanguard of a cultural revolution. Across other side of the Atlantic space, the final frontier was

being conquered. We'd seen the future, and many folk's appetite for it was unlimited. But what about Northampton? Could it become a town of tomorrow today?

In the late 1960s Northampton was described as 'an apple without a core'; it lacked the attraction of the major new shopping facilities beginning to be enjoyed by nearby towns. Moreover, in 1968, the town had been officially designated as a New Town, and was nominated for significant expansion to help cope with London's overspill. An increase in population from 130,000 to 230,000 was expected, though the figure was later scaled down to 180,000. Even so, the town centre facilities that already existed were quite inadequate to meet the demands of the expected huge increase in population.

Northampton County Borough Council swung into action to carry out a number of major redevelopments, one of which was the proposed new Grosvenor Shopping Centre. Five acres adjoining Abington Street and the Market Square were allocated to the scheme, which was eventually to regenerate the very heart of the town. The project was put into the hands of Grosvenor Estate Commercial Development Ltd, which had an enviable reputation as landowners in areas such as Mayfair and Belgravia. Its expertise in redevelopment work - including similar extensive under-cover shopping centres, reached across the country and overseas to Canada, Australia and other parts of the world. Grosvenor worked on the scheme in conjunction with the Post Office Pension Fund, which in the past had made significant investments in shopping developments in Corby, Stockton on Tees and Milton Keynes.

A key task was to establish the eventual cost and viability of the project: in-depth studies were carried out by Gleeds Quantity Surveyors. Numerous schemes were devised and costed; many were rejected, others were modified. At last the final design was arrived at and agreed. A list of contractors was compiled and invited to submit tenders to carry out the work.The contract for the building works was awarded to Wimpeys in April 1972, and they quickly began to clear the site earmarked for the new Centre.

Left: *Parade House, Market Square in 1880.*
Above: *An archaelogical dig which took place on the site in the 1970s.*

Work began with the demolition of the existing buildings, some of which had until then still been occupied, and with the clearing of two roads that were still in use across the site when work commenced. The site also contained the remains of an old friary which was at the time being explored by archaeologists. The entire operation needed careful co-ordination in order to give consideration to the occupiers and archaeologists, and the work was accordingly phased over five months.

When the site was eventually cleared an incredible 80,000 cubic metres of earth were then removed to make way for the foundations. Six tower cranes up to 150ft tall transported concrete to every part of the five acre site. As the new shopping centre grew, a small team of local stonemasons was engaged in the placing of hand-made facing bricks on certain of the elevations. All in all a total of 4,500 tons of reinforced concrete was used on the construction, and three million facing bricks were used on the external cladding of the building. The redevelopment plans included office space and car parking for a thousand cars as well as the enclosed two-tier shopping malls. In addition to the access staircases that link the malls, five passenger lifts were provided to serve the malls and car park above. With the continuing safety of the public in mind, the Centre was designed in consultation with the Northamptonshire Fire Service's Fire Prevention Officer, and many safety features

were incorporated into the design. A zoned fire alarm system was installed throughout the Centre, and an extensive sprinkler system, served by a large water storage tank housed in the car park entry ramp drum, formed a major part of the fire prevention arrangements. Each zone was individually relayed back to a panel situated in Management Control on the Service Deck. In turn this panel was designed to relay signals to the Fire Service headquarters, pinpointing an incident and even advising the Service which zone or entry point they should use in order to minimise delays.

Smoke detectors were positioned in each of the exhaust air plants to give early warning of any problems, and hose reels and fire hydrants were also installed around the Centre.

Should there be a power cut at any time, the Centre's automatic diesel generator was designed to immediately kick in to provide 50 percent emergency lighting in all the pedestrian areas and emergency power to ventilation plants and certain lifts. An air conditioning system was built into the design, to deliver around 50,000 cubic feet of fresh air every minute throughout the building, creating a controlled environment where shoppers would be able to browse in comfort around their favourite stores.

The creation of a shopping complex that was not only a useful facility, with access by pedestrian walkway directly from the bus station, but was at the same time attractive and comfortable to the shopping public was essential to the whole concept of adding life and sparkle to the town centre. Spaciousness without monotony was the aim of the architects, Stone Toms and Partners, and the resulting generously wide and stylishly designed shopping malls with large floor tiles and a marble finish to walls and columns were a tribute to their expertise. Column-free areas were provided at lower mall level. The clever variation in ceiling height throughout the building added to the feeling of depth and space, while the intensity of lighting in the malls, installed in recessed fittings, was kept to an intentionally low level to emphasise the individual lighting given out by each of the shop units.

Stone Toms designed The Friary on the upper mall, giving it vaulted ceilings, quarry tile flooring and effective concealed fluorescent lighting that lent a cloister-like feeling to the area. Positioned approximately above the excavated site of the old Greyfriars Monastery, The Friary was meant to ensure that this part of the town's rich history, excavated by archaeologists in 1970, would not be forgotten. The Friary became an attractive setting for the group of small shops set around an open café in the centre.

Facing page: *Work began on the site in the summer of 1972.* ***Above:*** *The Friary under construction.* ***Below:*** *The interior as it was in the late 1970s.*

Exciting and innovative, the shopping centre, built to a design that was still unusual when it was opened to the shopping public, was the combined result of all the painstaking planning of the numerous bodies involved in its conception, design and construction. The resulting facility is a credit to their various talents and expertise. The stylish Grosvenor Centre quickly became a source of pride and pleasure in the town - and remains so today.

The Centre's great attraction was that almost anything could be bought under one roof, and when it was opened stores such as Church's, Habitat, Waring and Gillow, Miss Selfridge, Boots, Sainsbury's, W H Smith, Saxone, Dixons and Beatties - to name only a few - provided people with a wide choice of goods from food to fashions and from photography to flowers.

Of course, there were grumbles. There always are when any new development takes place. Modernity was not to everyone's taste. Yet over the years the Grosvenor Centre acquired its own unique character, becoming a popular focal point where friends could meet and have a cup of coffee or something more substantial before doing the rounds of a huge choice of exciting shops and stores that range from large chain stores to small specialist retailers. Today, it is so much a part of the town that

The building fronted on to one of the most impressive market squares in the country, so the facade itself required careful planning to ensure that it was built in sympathy with the rest of Market Square. When it came to planning the outside, the Percy Thomas Partnership was brought in to assist Stone Toms in designing the Market Square frontage. The long history of the square goes back to Medieval times, and everyone involved in the planning recognised the importance of retaining the character of this unique and distinctive square while at the same time regenerating the area. It was quite a challenge.

To achieve architectural harmony, the rest of the buildings in the square had to be taken into consideration, and the architects carefully considered their heights and widths, roof profiles, window proportions and facing materials. Rebuilding of the sixteenth-century Welsh House, situated at the north-east corner of the square, formed an important part of the new development. Welsh House had for a long time been in very poor structural condition and had originally been earmarked for demolition. Happily, the authorities decided to retain and reconstruct the ancient building, keeping its original architectural character. The superbly recreated building was eventually occupied by Church's China Stores. Church's, probably the best known family business in Northampton, had moved into the town in 1858.

£80million

That's the asking price as Grosvenor Centre is put up for sale by current owners

Ambitious expansion plans could see town centre shopping complex double in size

BY JAMES TOZER

A MULTI-MILLION pound deal to double the size of Northampton's Grosvenor Centre is on the cards after the shopping complex was put up for sale.

■ Northampton's Grosvenor Centre is up for sale and is expected to fetch £80 million

Top left: *The Market Square facade in 1999.* ***Left:*** *An article that appeared in the local newspaper when the centre was offered for sale.*

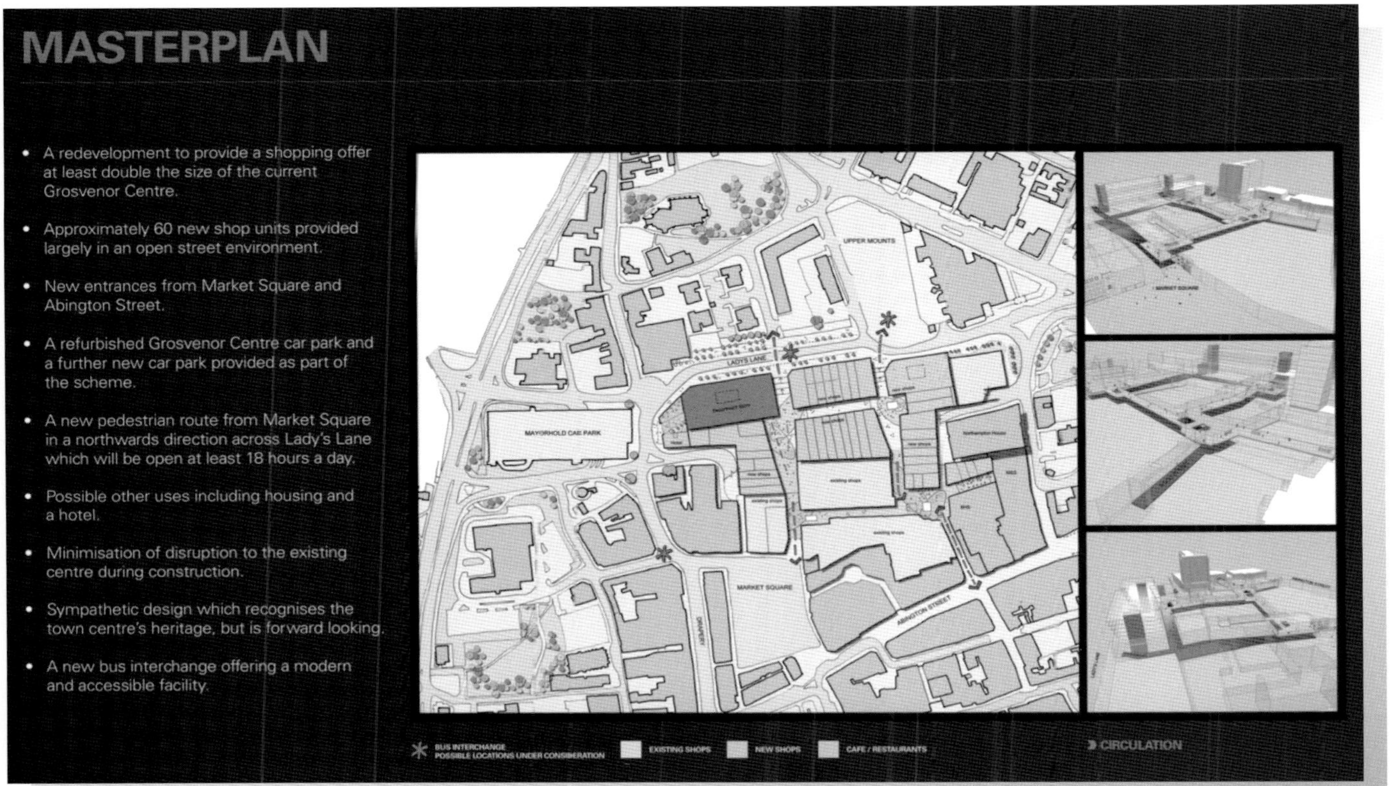

shoppers can scarcely imagine life without the Grosvenor Centre, which has truly become the core in the apple.

Further plans were soon afoot for the Centre's future. When Barclaycard vacated 150,000 square feet of office space in Greyfriars House in 1997 various options were discussed. Few business tenants were interested in moving in, and a scheme to convert the offices into more than 100 flats was considered and judged to be extremely difficult to bring about. The most likely option discussed was that of conversion to retail use, and property developers began discussing plans with Northampton Borough Council to expand the shopping facilities even further.

At the end of the 1990s Grosvenor Shopping Centre faced the new millennium with confidence, certain that whatever developments take place over the coming months and years, the Centre was assured of a future as exciting and innovative as its past.

Ten years later and plans were underway for a total redevelopment set to double the size of the Grosvenor Centre. The redevelopment plans drawn up in 2011 include no fewer than 60 new shops units, largely in an open street environment. New entrances to the Centre from the Market Square and Abington Street were now on the drawing board whilst the Grosvenor Centre car park would be refurbished and a further, new car park provided. A new pedestrian route from Market Square in a northwards direction was also planned across Lady's lane, open at least 18 hours a day.

Intrinsic to the redevelopment plans would be a new bus interchange offering far more modern and accessible service.

Perhaps most importantly of all, however, the redevelopment would call for a design which recognises the town centre's heritage whilst simultaneously being forward looking.

The Grosvenor Shopping Centre has become exactly what it promised to be so long ago: it is indeed the centre, the shopping heart of Northampton. What in the 1960s was strange and new has become for the generations born after it was built, normal, an integral part of the town as it has always been, rather than the novelty it was when it opened.

But, though it may have become an accepted part of the town centre, familiarity has never bred contempt. Today and for many decades yet to come the Grosvenor Shopping Centre is set to continue to fulfil its original promise, that of providing the most modern of shopping experiences, though still echoing our town's proud heritage.

Top: *Masterplan for Grosvenor Centre redevelopment.*

Westbridge Motors

A Long Road Travelled

The forecourt of Westbridge Motors, a few hundred yards from the town's railway station in St James Road, is a familiar sight to Northampton residents. It has served them, and many who have passed through the town, for over seven decades. As well as selling petrol it also provided car repair services from the large workshop at the rear.

Westbridge Motors is an independently owned and run family business established in 1937 and is well known for its 24-hour opening times and excellent service. As an independent company its aim is to always offer that little bit extra service to all its customers.

The company operates a 24-hour Vehicle Rescue and Recovery Division and has a 24-Hour BP Forecourt and Spar Convenience Store, where LPG gas is also offered as an alternative to traditional unleaded petrol.

In addition to its core services the firm also offers MOTs, servicing, exhausts, gearboxes, clutches, brakes and now tyres for any make of car or light commercial.

A fleet of Rescue and Recovery vehicles operate 24 hours a day, 365 days a year - they never close.

All these services are situated at the company's centrally located site in Northampton and easily accessible from the M1. The Rescue and Recovery division also operates from another depot situated in the south of the county.

Westbridge Motors was founded by John Brocklehurst and his brother Cecil in 1937, and in the mid sixties the management was handed over to John's two sons, Robert and Nick. In 1998 Nick's son Karl, joined the company, Nick and Karl run the company today.

It was perhaps not the best time to choose to start such a business. On the outbreak of war in 1939, the garage was closed and designated as an emergency mortuary to be used should Northampton experience large-scale air raids. After the war, when things began to return to normal, the garage reopened, first selling 'pool' petrol, but shortly many old and well-remembered names appeared on the pumps, including 'Power', 'National Benzol', 'Shellmex' and 'BP'.

The business expanded its scope of operations when John's brother-in-law, Geoff Pakes, joined in 1946 and started the Westbridge Private Hire and Taxi Service, operating with two Humber Snipes. It was his custom to sleep on the premises and this was the start of the Westbridge commitment to 24-hour service which has been a feature of the firm ever since.

Top left: *Company founder John Brocklehurst.* ***Left:*** *Filling a car in post-war austerity, 1947.* ***Above:*** *One of the company's early taxis.*

The years between the end of the Second World War and the 1960s saw the car change from being a luxury means of transport only for the rich and famous to an everyday necessity for many - a trend which continues today. Two-car households are commonplace and four-car households not so rare nowadays, so the Westbridge line of business was one in which the opportunities were extensive and consumer expectations were steadily increasing.

In 1962, Robert Brocklehurst joined the company as an engineering apprentice, later taking responsibility for all engineering matters and continuing the family involvement. He was joined by his brother Nick two years later, who took on responsibility for the parts department and increasingly for the retail side of things, which included the major growth area of the forecourt.

When the M1 motorway was opened, the Westbridge 24-hour Breakdown and Recovery Service was launched to cater for the problems encountered by motorists who found that their cars were not up to travelling at sustained high speeds. This proved to be a highly successful development in the business, and today Westbridge are agents for a number of the major breakdown recovery services.

John Brocklehurst went into semi-retirement in 1972, and though he and his wife, Evelyn, remained shareholders and retained a keen interest in the company's fortunes, the day-to-day running of the company fell to their sons, Robert and Nick helped and supported by their wives, Heather and Erika.

The early 1970s saw the younger generation seize new opportunities to take the business forward. One such opening was when the eastern adjacent site came up for sale. This was quickly purchased. It meant that the position of the garage could become much more prominent and visible to the general public. This led to the redesign of the Shell forecourt which came in 1973 and incorporated the then new concept of self-service and shop facilities as well as improving access for traffic on the busy St James Road. This forward-looking approach has continued over the years and amongst other innovations led to the

Above: *An aerial view of the site in 1947.* ***Below:*** *Westbridge Motors circa 1949/50.*

introduction of the Westbridge Charge Card, valued by many for the speedy way it enabled transactions to go through.

Along with the newly acquired land came a four-storey bonded warehouse. A major distiller approached the brothers asking whether they would be prepared to continue to offer the facility to provide warehousing facilities for it, and this further opportunity to expand and diversify was seized.

Geoff Pakes set about acquiring the necessary license from Customs and Excise and learning about this specialised trade. Though they went into it on a trial basis and found it hard going at first, it became a thriving concern. It couldn't operate without the computerised system which allows calculations of the precise excise duty payable - this is a complicated process which has to take into account all relevant UK and European legislation. During the national lorry drivers' strike in 1977 the bonded store brought into use its own transport to distribute whisky to the distillers' customers in East Anglia. There were so many compliments on their speed and efficiency that they were asked to continue the service, which they were very pleased to do.

With this increased activity it became apparent, especially with the introduction of VAT, that it was necessary to recruit the services of a person responsible for the administration of the office procedures. In 1975 the company was fortunate in obtaining the services of Alan Wilson, who previously worked for a local firm of accountants, to take over the day-to-day administration and oversight of the company's ever-increasing paper work and legal requirements. Alan was appointed Director in 1977.

Another significant development took place soon after Bernard Smith joined the company as a taxi controller. He realised that second-hand mechanically tested parts on an 'off-the-shelf' basis would prove to be a valuable service, not only to customers, but also to insurance companies who had badly damaged cars to dispose of. So Westbridge Motors now became vehicle dismantlers, employing a team of

Above: *Westbridge Motors in the 1960s.* ***Below:*** *A former Westbridge recovery vehicle.*

professionals to strip parts from second-hand cars for steam cleaning and mechanical testing before being sold at one-third of the new part price. The cars were brought in by Westbridge's own recovery service - an ideal way of solving the insurance companies' problem of disposing of badly damaged vehicles and at the same time re-using the undamaged parts, providing a useful service to the public.

A talking point among many Northampton residents and a familiar sight to Westbridge customers was now the 'half a car' which was created as a promotional idea and also shown at local carnivals.

More space was created by the acquisition in 1984 of three-quarters of an acre to the west of the Westbridge premises, and the Used Car Parts Department and the Breakdown Service were relocated there.

In 1992, however, due to changes in insurance companies' policies, the used car parts business was sold to a larger operator, Auto Spares and Salvage, of Rushden, and the building used for the expansion of the breakdown department with the balance converted into small workshop units.

On the occasion of Geoff Pakes' retirement in 1983, Bernard Smith was appointed director with responsibility for the bonded warehouse and distribution side of the business.

In 1987 the bond again increased in size and the firm leased an additional 20,000 square feet of warehouse space and gained a major new contract in distribution using Tautliner Scania 16 tonne vehicles designed to facilitate the needs of the operation. However, with the changing market place and EEC regulations the Bond closed in 1990.

In the 1980s the company took on the licences of three Shell sites, namely Cattlemarket Filling Station, Paulersbury Self Serve and, in 1986, a new forecourt concept by Shell called Travellers Check on the A508 at Wootton, a site opened by Noel Edmunds, and operated until 1997.

The Company celebrated its 50th anniversary in 1987 by having a stand at the Northampton Show at which staff showed some of the facets of their organisation and, among other things, held a balloon race - all profits from which went to the hospital CAT Scanner appeal.

At Easter 1998 the site was affected by the Northampton flood and was under three feet of water but still managed to keep trading throughout the difficult period.

Top left: *The firm's half-car used to promote the Westbridge Spare Parts centre.* ***Above left:*** *Robert and Nick Brocklehurst.* ***Below:*** *The flooded forecourt in 1998.*

(Autogas), and it was decided to include a pump on the new forecourt, the first one on a BP forecourt in England.

A new conveyor car wash opened in 2001 capable of washing a car every minute, the first of its type in Northampton. Customer requirements, however, changed – they demanded a more individual approach. The hand wash arrived. The conveyer wash was modified and the nylon brushes removed.

With the knowledge gained in operating the Shell new concept site and following the acquisition of half an acre of land from the adjoining plot of land owned by Travis Perkins, a major redevelopment of the site started in August 1998, to build a modern forecourt with the latest technology together with a 2,000 square feet convenience store. Nick's son Karl joined the company to manage the new facility, which opened in December 1998, and was shortly joined by his sister Annabel. The facility continues the Westbridge commitment to 24-hour service. The store offers a large selection of convenience goods including confectionery, soft drinks, car care and a wide range of food to include hot and cold snacks, sandwiches and ready meals. This was added to in 2000 when a licence was obtained to sell alcohol and spirits, wines and beers. They have also benefited from having parking in front of the store making it easier for customers to shop, especially for those heavy items such as coal and gas.

When the redevelopment was carried out Karl's vision for the future proposed the inclusion of a new type of auto fuel, LPG

A powerful six-hose vacuum cleaner system was installed to clean the inside of vehicles. Under-chassis washing, rinsing and liquid waxing and drying would still be carried out by machinery, but with the 'crew' detailing each vehicle to a high standard.

In 2006 Westbridge Motors filling station receive an award from William Reed, publishers of Forecourt Trader magazine. Westbridge Motors was voted 'Forecourt Trader of the Year'. The award was decided by a panel of experts travelling the length of the country in search of the best facilities and services being offered by independent filling station operators. The presentation took place in the Hilton Hotel, in Park Lane, London.

The spotlight immediately focussed on the site. A major supermarket chain made approaches to the family about buying the

Top left and top right: *View of Westbridge Motors in 1973 (top left) and 1998 (top right).* ***Left:*** *Westbridge Motors' valeting service area.* ***Above:*** *Karl Brocklehurst pictured with the 'Forecourt Trader of the Year' award in 2006.*

site. The family decided it was in their best interests, however, to enter into a long lease arrangement with their existing Spar wholesaler, AF Blakemore & Son, and allow them to manage the retail fuel and convenience store operations.

Meanwhile, under the leadership of Karl Brocklehurst, the recovery business was expanding. New contracts were acquired from many of the national breakdown recovery organisations, insurance companies and many local car dealerships. The fleet of recovery vehicles rapidly increased to 17.

In 2007 Westbridge Recovery purchased another long-established family recovery business, Freeways Motors of Weedon. To service the increased area a new recovery depot, Northampton South, was set up on the A5 midway between Towcester and Weedon. Today, the recovery operation rescues stranded motorists throughout the county, and in 2008 even undertook, for one of their clients, the recovery of a stranded commercial vehicle in the south of France, bringing it back to the owner's depot in the UK.

The 24-hour private hire taxi business had also grown steadily to 47 cars from its inception in 1947, with just two vehicles. It was, however, sold in October 2011 to Bounds Taxis (Northampton) Ltd, a well-known and long-established local private hire operator.

Elsewhere, the family has enlarged its real estate, from half an acre in 1937 to its current 2.2 acre site. Many other well known local businesses are tenants, such as Frog Island brewery run by Bruce and Mandy Littler, Mutiny Hair and Beauty run by Jo Caswell, Audio works sound recording studio operated by Josh Astrop, and Quills Leisure run by Marc Sawer, selling Quad bikes and motorcycles, plus five other businesses, leasing and operating workshop units. These are, Leroy Moven, Paul Slinn, John Howard, G&W Autos, and JSB Auto Electricians.

As for the future, Westbridge Motors Ltd will undoubtedly continue to respond to changing customer needs and develop new business opportunities, continuing a fine tradition established for over seven decades.

Top and above left: *Part of the Westbridge Motors' fleet of recovery vehicles.* ***Left:*** *Nick and Karl Brocklehurst, 2011.* ***Below:*** *A bird's eye view of Westbridge Motors' St James Road premises.*

Stantone Mechanical Handling - Raising the Bar

When Stantone Mechanical Handling Ltd celebrated its half century in business in 2011 it was not only marking an important anniversary in its own history but also its part in the history of industry throughout Northamptonshire.

Stantone Mechanical Handling Limited, based in Rothersthorpe Avenue, Far Cotton, Northampton, is one of the largest forklift companies in Northamptonshire, and is the official Clark/Samsung lift truck distributor in the area. Over more than 50 years in business the company has developed an unrivalled reputation for quality, service and reliability. Stantone staff genuinely want to assist in solving clients' handling problems whether this calls for a casual hire truck during a busy period, or for designing a piece of equipment for a specific task. The company can also give advice and provide flexible methods of financing equipment on either Contract Hire or Hire Purchase.

Formed in 1961 by Stan Hall and Tony Smith, Northampton-based Stantone - the company title combining Stan and Tony's names - at first specialised in crane hire. The business thrived, responding to the needs of the publicly owned gas and steel industries, particularly in Corby. The Stantone teams were involved in the construction of some of the area's largest industrial estates.

Over the years, adapting to its market, Stantone moved away from crane and skip hire to concentrate on hiring out fork lift trucks.

People have always looked for easier ways of doing difficult lifting jobs. Stonehenge can only have been constructed using some method of raising those great stones. No doubt our Bronze Age ancestors made use of the lever. Famously, however, it was the Ancient Greek scientist Archimedes who finally recognised the mechanical principle on which the lever worked, famously saying "Give me but one firm spot on which to stand and I will move the earth". But there is no doubt whatsoever that the long-ago builders of the pyramids, Stonehenge and the Parthenon would have been more pleased to have a single fork lift truck than any number of levers.

Top: *Founders, Stan Hall (left) and Tony Smith.* ***Left:*** *Stan (right) and Tony standing by a 1942 Coles crane.* ***Above:*** *A Coles crane at the company's Haringstone depot in 1961.*

It was not until the 19th century that basic, manually-powered sack trucks were developed; the idea was so good that they are still used to this day. Inevitably human ingenuity was applied to the idea and other types of hand operated equipment were developed; platform trucks and four wheeled trailers, for example. At the beginning of the 20th century new versions of these trucks began to appear driven by electric motors powered by batteries.

In the USA the Pennsylvania Railroad introduced battery powered platform trucks for moving luggage at their Altoona, Pennsylvania, train station in 1906. Health and safety was definitely not a consideration back in those days, but they did assist in getting the job done and later models were made with a platform which could be raised and lowered electrically.

The Clark company in the USA is credited with producing the forerunner of the seated counterbalanced truck in 1917; but it was its competitor, Yale, that, in 1925, produced the first electric truck that had raising forks and an elevating mast. No tilt was fitted to the machine and the lift was by ratchet and pinion as hydraulic systems had not been incorporated into trucks at that time. It was difficult to drive: the operator stood upright on two large, spring loaded wooden blocks which were used to change direction.

Above: *Part of the Hydrocon fleet at Rothersthorpe Avenue depot in the mid-1960s.* ***Below:*** *Tony Smith (left) and Stan Hall (second left) take delivery of a new Hydrocon crane in the 1960s.*

The advent of First World War in 1914 would make the fork lift truck popular, mainly due to the shortage of labour. World War I saw the development of different types of material handling equipment in the United Kingdom by Ransomes, Sims and Jeffries of Ipswich. In 1917 Clark in the United States began developing and using powered tractor and powered lift tractors in their factories.

Following the war's end in 1918 the truck designers decided that putting loads on top of each other would be rather a good idea, and so a high lift version of the platform truck was produced for the first time.

In 1919 the Towmotor Company, and Yale & Towne Manufacturing in 1920, entered the lift truck market in the United States.

Continuing development and expanded use of the forklift continued through the 1920s and 1930s. World War II, like World War I before, spurred the use of forklift trucks in the war effort. Many of these trucks would be brought to the United Kingdom in the early 1940s by the USA's armed forces based in Britain for the war effort.

July 1966

HYDROCON NEWS

PUBLISHED BY LAMBERT ENGINEERING CO. (GLASGOW) LIMITED

'HEY DAD CAN WE HAVE ONE OF THESE?'

Story: Next page

A 1926 Yale truck from the USA is believed to be the oldest surviving fork lift in the world. It is now on display at the National Fork Truck Heritage Centre, based at the Midlands Railway Centre at Butterley, near Derby.

British industry was slow to take up the idea of the lift truck, but the outbreak of the Second World War in 1939 and the consequent shortage of labour soon made them indispensable for loading vast quantities of war goods onto wagons and ships. The era of the fork lift tuck had finally arrived.

After the war's end in 1945, more efficient and economic methods for storing products in warehouses were being developed – not least using space more effectively by storing goods overhead. Warehouses needed more manoeuvrable forklift trucks that could reach greater heights. New forklift models were made that filled the need to lift goods ever higher.

British industry had begun importing large numbers of fork lift trucks from the USA before the war but they were used mainly for outdoor work. However, in 1946 the British firm, Coventry Climax, produced the first ever British fork lift truck; its 1949 'Coventry Climax' truck would become legendary.

One company that had a very significant impact on the UK truck industry was Lansing Bagnall who took the counterbalanced truck, redesigned it and produced the world's first reach truck for use in narrow aisle applications.

Nowadays, trucks are more sophisticated with complicated electronic and hydraulic systems,

Above: *Robert and David Hall appear on the cover of the July 1996 Hydrocon News publication.* ***Below:*** *Robert and David alongside a Hydrocon Crane in the late 1960s.*

high visibility masts and with comfort and safety for the operator paramount.

Meanwhile, the ever inventive Japanese were not far behind. Toyota introduced its first lift truck model, the Model LA, in Japan in 1956. A decade later Toyota exported its first forklift to the United States where it had been invented.

Basingstoke-based Lansing Bagnall and Co Ltd. (now part of the German firm Linde), is generally credited with inventing the moving mast reach truck in 1954. Regarded as a marvel in its day, this truck allowed operators to stack goods and operate in aisles that were much narrower than before and to stack loads far higher too.

In warehouses a typical aisle width was 2.5m. This has led in modern times to high density warehouses with very narrow aisles. The idea was a truck with a mast that retracted towards the operator for stability during normal travel but could be extended beyond the wheelbase in order to deposit and retrieve the load.

Most narrow aisle trucks were developed from this single principle including both man-down and man-up combi-trucks which are now so common and which were also invented by Lansing Bagnall.

Several other companies have laid claim to the invention of the reach truck, but since Linde is said to hold the original patent such claims appear unfounded.

In the meantime, another key development had taken place in parallel with the fork lift truck: the wooden pallet.

Wooden skids had long been used for moving goods about. In 1925, however, the addition of bottom boards to such skids resulted in the very first pallet.

The natural partnership between pallets and forklifts quickly provided a much faster turnaround for railway wagons and ships. According to an article in a 1931 railway trade magazine, three days were needed to unload a railway wagon containing 13,000 cases of unpalletised canned goods. When the same amount of goods were loaded into a carriage using pallets or skids, the job took only four hours.

Top left: *A Stantone crane on hire in Nipton in the 1960s.* ***Left:*** *Reconditioning a Ministry of Defence crane in 1967.* ***Above:*** *A paint job for Blackwood Hodge.*

The earliest record of large scale pallet production was the NEPA Pallet company of Snohomish, Washington State. NEPA was certainly the first pallet manufacturing business of any size. It was formed in 1937 by Walter Crook together with three partners to meet a US government contract to supply 'dock boards' or 'stevedore pallets'.

Pallets, and the consequential standardisation of load sizes, would in turn lead to far greater efficiency in goods distribution and storage – something which would in itself contribute greatly to the war effort against Hitler and Nazi Germany.

More than seventy years on, war is far from most folk's minds. But in a sense, commerce too is war, with all the excitement, but happily none of its bloodshed.

When the current directors of Stantone, Richard Barkworth and Robert Hall (the latter the son of founder Stan Hall), bought the company in 2002 it was with a view to waging a renewed commercial battle to grow the sales side of the business, and their intentions have certainly been realised.

"I started working here in 1974, three years after my father passed away and I learned my trade as an apprentice engineer", says Robert Hall.

Stan Hall passed away in 1971. Tony Smith continued to run the business and in 1972/3 the crane side of the business was sold though the firm continued to service and repair cranes as well as selling them.

Crane load testing was also a large part of the company.

Robert Hall started at Stantone in 1974 to carry out a full apprenticeship in crane and plant maintenance.

During this apprenticeship time was spent at Northampton Diesel and Electrical Ltd to gain knowledge in those fields.

Above: *Since 2001 Stantone Mechanical Handling has provided a free Clark forklift truck and other floor conveyor equipment to the 'Vulcan To The Sky Trust' team. The team got together in 1997 to put together a plan to return the Vulcan to the sky after being grounded since 1993. With over £7million spent the Vulcan took to the air again in 2007. Pictured are Stantone's Directors Robert Hall (left) and Richard Barkworth (right).* ***Left:*** *Stantone's Nathan Gardner receives a certificate for Employee of the Year at the National Forklift Truck Association awards in 2010. He was nominated by Richard Barkworth and Robert Hall in recognition of his hard-working attitude and dedication to the job.* ***Below:*** *Refurbished trucks awaiting delivery to Dalepack Nipton, July 2011.*

Northampton Diesel and Electrical Ltd was a company formed by Stan and Tony at Unit 3 which it soon outgrew and had to relocate. The company continued to repair, test and service cranes, plant and fork lift trucks all over the United Kingdom including steel works and power stations. This continued into the late 1980s when the business moved over to fork lift trucks and road transport of plant and fork lift trucks.

The late Tony Smith retired in the 1990s and the company was then run by Alan J. Ferguson until 2001.

Richard Barkworth joined the company in 2000; he and Robert Hall took over the company in 2001 when Alan Ferguson retired.

"When the opportunity arose to buy the company with Richard from the then owner Alan Ferguson I jumped at the chance and we have worked hard to make the company one of the leading forklift specialists in the area," say Robert Hall.

The company offers sales, contract and lease hire, maintenance and service; it also provides a range of major brands in the mechanical handling sector including Clark, Nexen, Samsung and Crown. It is an accredited Lolar inspection centre and undertakes driver training.

"Things were ticking over steadily in 2002 but there was no-one really going out there to grow the business which was something we wanted to change," says Richard Barkworth.

"Today the majority of our customers choose contract hire because they don't have any worries; they know we're just a phone call away if they need repairs, service or want to update their products. We also deal with sales, casual hire and the service, maintenance and repairs side of the business.

"Both Robert and I have worked as engineers and can speak to customers with confidence about the products, rather than simply being sales people. I think they know they can trust us because of that. Then we have a team of four engineers who are out on the road providing a fast quality service to all our customers."

In 2006, Stantone bought the Bedfordshire-based company Jem Handling having been approached by the owner because of his belief that his company would be in the safe hands of the team at Stantone.

"He knew us through the business and knew we would carry on in his business in the way he wanted and look after his customers the way he would have done, and we still have some of those customers today," says Richard "We're proud of our personal, traditional approach and that we have successfully passed our 50th anniversary milestone."

Today, more than half a century on from when the company was founded in 1961, Stantone Mechanical Handling Ltd is now a specialist forklift truck company, providing service, maintenance, sales and contract hire facilities for new and used vehicles. The company has a fleet of 100 forklift trucks, and is a main dealer for Samsung, Nissan, Crown Warehouse Equipment Diesel Side Loaders, and more recently became a fully qualified agent for the servicing and maintenance of Pyroban Trucks.

Above: *Stantone Mechanical's Rothersthorpe Avenue premises.* ***Below:*** *Directors, Richard Barkworth (left) and Robert Hall.*

Moulton College

Innovation and Excellence in Teaching and Learning

In 2011 Moulton College celebrated its 90th anniversary. The College's Alumni now form a network of over 10,000 professionals, with new graduates adding to their numbers every year.

Moulton College, formerly Northamptonshire Farm Institute, was opened in 1921 and, with the exception of the war years, has been training students of all ages ever since.

Originally the Institute comprised Home Farm (now the Holcot Centre) and property in West Street – two detached houses and four cottages for farm staff.

One of the houses was occupied by the Principal; the other provided a dining room and common room for students as well as accommodation for staff. In the grounds, two wooden buildings provided bedrooms for students in addition to a lecture room and laboratory.

The Institute afforded excellent facilities for the investigation of farming problems and served as an experimental station; it also offered instruction to rural teachers. By 1930, however, it was clear that better buildings were needed and in 1933 Mrs A S Harrison donated Red Hill Farm, Wellingborough, along with £10,000 towards the building of a 'new institute' which included a hostel for 40 students and further lecture rooms.

Above: *The 1930s Northamptonshire Farm Institute.* ***Below:*** *Students on the College estate in 1934.*

Following an unsatisfactory inspection by HMIs, the 1960s was a decade of recovery and growth for the Institute with a new teaching wing, (now the Learning Resources Centre) a demonstration kitchen, staff offices and accommodation for 100 students (now demolished and replaced by the Higher Education Centre) together with a new common room and library (now the Student Welfare Centre) being added.

The Thomas Harrison Farm was absorbed into the Wellingborough Town scheme to accommodate London overspill population and was replaced by the Moulton Lodge Farm (now the Management Centre) and Stud Farm (now the Pitsford Centre).

In 1966 the Institute became a College after the Pilkington Report suggested that 'the county agricultural establishments calling themselves schools or institutes set themselves apart from technical colleges to no particular purpose.'

With the outbreak of war in 1939 all traditional courses were cancelled. The first wartime course for Women's Land Army trainees began on 18 September, 1939, and continued throughout the war. In all, some 1,300 women received training at the Institute. In addition to providing training for the WLA, staff were also actively involved in encouraging the work of the Women's Institute Produce Guild and the County Allotment Holders to increase home production of food.

The famous 'Dig for Victory' slogan was taken very literally, and wartime food shortages would undoubtedly have been far worse had it not been for the practical help and encouragement given by the Institute. Herr Hitler must have been told, as the work of the Institute was not helped when in October 1941 the site was bombed by the Luftwaffe!

The first Principal was Walter Stewart, who, astonishingly, did not retire until 1958 after almost 38 years of service. Under his direction the Institute had become known both nationally and internationally.

The late 1970s and 1980s were disappointing periods for the College. Student numbers tailed off, there was insufficient investment in the estate, and a failure to diversify the curriculum. In 1988/9 Moulton enrolled only 46 full-time students.

The 1992 'Further and Higher Education Act' freed Colleges from local authority control and Moulton became independent.

Fortunately, Moulton flourished as an independent college and its mission was broadened as it sought to become 'a Centre of Excellence for education and training for the land-based, construction and furniture industries'.

Top left: *Agricultural students at Fat Stock Show, Christmas 1933.* ***Above:*** *Students maintaining equipment in the 1950s.* ***Left:*** *Students taking part in a pageant in 1955.*

The Governing Body approved an ambitious investment programme and throughout the 1990s standards of learning and teaching steadily improved. The College also gained 'Investor in People', 'Careermark', and 'Basic Skills Agency Quality Mark' accreditation.

In 2004, a joint inspection by Ofsted and the Adult Learning Inspectorate (ALI) judged the College to be 'Outstanding', and to 'provide Good Value for Money'. However, it was in October 2004 that Moulton was delivered the ultimate accolade when it was the first land-based college in the country to be awarded 'Learning and Skills Beacon' status by the Department for Education and Skills.

The Learning and Skills Council (LSC) featured Moulton as a case study in 2007 within its 'Success for All' report, stating that: "The College has focused on meeting the needs of its employers, many of whom see it as the first choice provider. The College's atmosphere oozes professionalism in all that it does".

Following inspection by Ofsted in 2008, the College was once again judged to be 'Outstanding' and to provide 'Outstanding Value for Money.' In 2009, a Care Standards inspection by Ofsted judged the College to be 'Outstanding' under every category. A more recent Quality Assurance Agency inspection of higher education courses awarded the College its highest accolade possible, recognising the management of quality and standards of higher education courses.

The College's growing success provided the Governing Body with the confidence to further develop the campus, and between 1994 and 2011 more than £60million was invested to provide some of the best practical teaching resources in the country. Vocational Skills Academies were established in East Northants., South Northants., and Daventry. Direct funding was secured from the Higher Education Funding Council, enabling the College to develop a wide range of undergraduate courses with progression up to doctorate level.

The College now offers a unique range of programmes to enhance its status as a 'Centre of Excellence providing

Education and Training for the Natural, Built and Recreational Environment', and prepares students for qualifications ranging from pre-entry, further education up to doctorate level.

Chris Moody, who was the Principal of the College, retired in January of 2011 after some 18 years in post and has been followed by Stephen M Davies.

Under the experienced eye of Stephen Davies, the College will continue to offer the very best opportunities for young people. In 2011, with so many students being successful in their chosen subject, there were seven awards ceremonies, each celebrating

Left: *Former Principal, Chris Moody presenting NVQ Level 3 certificates in Construction to Daniel Kellock and Samantha Stone in 1999.* ***Above:*** *Countryside Management students.* ***Below:*** *The Wilson Countryside Management Centre, opened in 2011.*

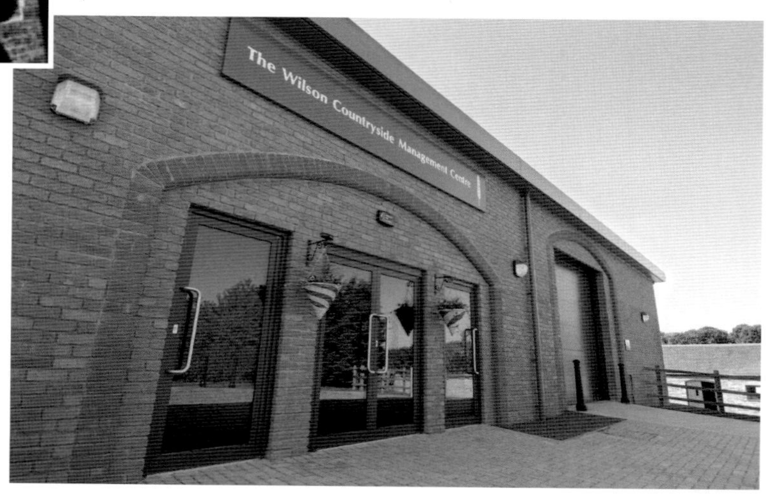

achievement in a specific subject area. Based on the Government success factor measurements for 16-18-year-olds, who make up the majority of students, Moulton's results put it in the top 1% of all further education providers, of which there are around 700.

During 2010/11, the College enrolled more than 3,200 full-time and 4,000 part-time students at its various sites. Add to this around 800 secondary school pupils from over 50 schools, who attend for a day or a half day each week, plus more than 2,000 primary school children from around 40 schools who have attended courses at the Holdenby Centre, and one gets some impression of the volume of activity. To deliver that range of services, Moulton now employs over 800 staff and has a turnover of more than £28million, making it one of the largest

employers in the district and one that makes a significant contribution to the local economy which is projected to be £26 billion over the next two decades. New projects are in hand which include building the new £6million Social Centre for staff and students on the college's main site opening in early 2012. This building will provide a wide range of social and leisure facilities for both staff and students including new dining areas, bar, lounge, games area, under-18s area, TV lounge, information study, HE learning support, student welfare, nurse, counselling and chaplaincy all under one roof.

The construction of a new £8.5million Sports Therapy and Injury Rehabilitation Centre at the Pitsford Centre was completed in January 2012 in readiness to provide outstanding teaching facilities for students and support services for the Olympics, professional and amateur sports teams and individual sportsmen and women. This unique facility in the UK incorporates specialist teaching facilities and a comprehensive sports rehabilitation suite/clinic to provide students with opportunities to develop experience in a clinic run by sports therapy professionals, and a 25-metre swimming pool. The swimming pool is to be used for teaching, therapeutic and recreational purposes and will also be available for use by the wider community.

The Wilson Countryside Management Centre at South Lodge was opened in September 2011 housing specialist fish management, game-keeping and countryside skill workshops. The dining room and ground floor of Stewart House and Thomas Harrison Hostel have been converted back to their earlier use with the creation of five new lecture rooms, access to the first floor by lift and improvements to the exterior of the building.

Further development is planned with the creation of a new improved reception and student services during 2012.

Nine decades after establishment in its permanent home in Moulton village, the College still pursues excellence, whilst continuing to offer opportunity to those who have not previously tasted success or achieved formal qualifications.

Above left: *The Learning Resource Centre, opened in 2009.* ***Top Right:*** *The Chris Moody Sports Therapy and Injury Rehabilitation Centre, 2012.* ***Above:*** *Principal, Stephen M Davies, 2011.* ***Below:*** *The Moulton College Social Centre, 2012.*

Weston Favell Shopping Centre

Past, Present and Future

Known in the 11th century as Westone, and as Weston Fauvelle in the 13th century, Weston Favell can trace its history as far back as the Domesday Book of 1086. The famous book provides evidence of the overlordship of the village and surrounding area first being awarded to the Count of Mortain. The area subsequently passed through the families of Mundeville and d'Avranches into the possession of the Crevecoeurs, under whom the lord of the manor was then John Fauvelle, hence the name Weston Favell.

The manorial lordship continued in the Fauvelle family until the death of Sir William Favell without heirs, around 1316, when it passed into the Griffin family. The name of the village, however, remained unchanged.

The present church building can be dated to a similar early period. Indeed, the tower is of the late 12th century, of 'Transitional Norman' style, whilst the chancel belongs mainly to the first half of the 13th century, being a rebuilding of an earlier 12th-century chancel, the original priest's doorway of which was retained.

In the intervening centuries Weston Favell has changed greatly: not least since its larger neighbour Northampton has grown to meet it.

Commentators in 1931 noted how much the population had grown – the parish by then having a population of 1,094!

Then in 1965 Northampton was designated a new town which led to a huge expansion of its population. Many Londoners emigrated to Northampton. A Development Corporation was formed in 1968 and building work began in 1970. The first new area to be built was the Eastern District followed in the late 1970s and early 1980s by the Western District.

When planning permission was applied for in 1972 to turn an area of undeveloped wasteland near Weston Favell into a new shopping centre, few could have visualised the eventual outcome - a lively, bustling facility with a quarter of a million square feet of climatically controlled shopping area, and parking space, both outdoor and undercover, for more than 1,000 vehicles. With Gordon Redfern in charge of the centre's design, work on Phase 1 of the Weston Favell Shopping Centre soon got underway.

Meanwhile, new houses meant an opportunity not only for new shops but

Left: *Construction work began on the Weston Favell Shopping Centre in June 1972.*

also for new churches. Church leaders in 1970 decided not to build their own individual churches but to work together in one building on the edge of the proposed new shopping centre. Today Emmanuel Church is still in the Weston Favell shopping centre: with one entrance beyond the library and another in the bus bay for the Centre.

When the centre was officially opened on 29th October, 1974, by Baroness Evelyn Sharp building work was still going on outside. Inside, it was a different story. Pleasantly light and cheerful, the spacious enclosed shopping area immediately put the VIPs attending the opening ceremony at their ease. Baroness Sharp, who had been Permanent Secretary at the Ministry of Housing and Development, confessed in her speech that initially she had had some doubts about how well the Development Corporation and the Borough Council would work closely together on the project; the reality, however, had far exceeded her hopes. Dr John Weston, General Manager of the Northampton Development

Above: *An early view of South Square and Main Mall.* ***Below:*** *The shopping centre with the suburbs of Northampton behind in a picture dating from 1977.*

Corporation, was forced to attend the ceremony in a wheelchair. An unfortunate accident while on holiday in the Lake District had resulted in a broken leg - and presented him with a golden opportunity to put the centre's wheelchair ramps to the test!

The centre was home to a huge Tesco superstore, by far Tesco's biggest development, exceeding by 22,000 square feet the previous largest, in Stevenage. The group's firm declaration was to make this branch of Tescos one of the most successful in the world. Lines of shopping trolleys, as yet unused, waited inside the doors for the store's first shoppers. The trolleys cost around £20 each - a daunting sum of money 25 years ago. The invention of the £1 slot to ensure the safe return of shopping trolleys was still some way in the future!

Shopping in a facility sheltered from cold winds and driving rain held great appeal. The temperature-controlled environment that was snugly comfortable in the howling winds of winter was also a cool refuge from the hot sun of summer. The upper shopping mall was built with a high barrel-vaulted ceiling that allowed natural light to filter through along its 180 metre length, giving the impression of browsing in an old traditional shopping arcade. The arcaded mall played its own part in making the new Weston Favell Centre popular with the majority of Northampton's shopping public. A lower shopping mall ran alongside the entire length of the undercover parking facilities.

In addition to the huge number of shops of every kind, including Boots and W H Smith, the centre offered the benefits of two major supermarkets, with Supacentre being housed there as well as the large Tesco store. There was little need for shoppers to go elsewhere, as linked by a series of ramps, escalators, autowalks and lifts, around fifty shops and stores made sure that most if not all of their needs could be supplied under one roof. Ladies' fashions, menswear, knitting wools, haberdashery and supplies for the handicraft enthusiast, books, gifts, toiletries and medication - all were there to offer their tempting wares to the buyer. And when shoppers had 'shopped till they dropped' they could take their weary feet into the nearest coffee shop to snatch a quick cuppa or enjoy a more substantial meal; both supermarkets offered cafeterias as part of their service. The centre also had other services such as banks, building societies, a post office and a library on the premises, while the Emmanuel Church catered for the spiritual needs of the people.

Over the intervening years ownership of the centre has changed hands a number of times. In 1984 Capital and Counties Shopping Centres took over the ownership of the centre with Bob Baldry appointed as Centre

Top: *Weston Favell Shopping Centre celebrated St Valentines Day 2007 in style with the return of Flavia and Vincent from BBC's 'Strictly Come Dancing'.* ***Above:*** *Jems Hip Hop troop show the kids a few moves.*

Manager. Capital and Counties sold the businesses to Pillar Caisse in September 1994, which in turn sold to Tesco British Land Partnership in 1997. During these periods the Centre was managed by Chris Fenn and Nick Smith.

During Tesco British Land Partnership's tenure and management by Sharon Carter planning permission was granted for a further 70,000 square foot of retail space as well as a petrol filling station to be built. This formed the southern end extension to the centre and was completed and opened to the public in October 2002.

This bright and modern addition to the shopping scene in Northampton was welcomed by the public with increased visits bringing in further custom to both the existing and new tenants, who by this time totaled over 65.

Many of those additions, like Wilkinson's, Peacocks and Savers, complemented the existing national retailers as well as the many local independent traders that make up the varied range of shops still on offer today.

In January 2006 a new Centre Manager was appointed, Kevin Legg, who was in place when in August of that year Tesco British Land Partnership sold the centre to Northampton Holding Ltd. Northampton Holding Ltd remain the current landlords and it is under their ownership that we have seen the centre continue to develop and prosper with further and a more diverse offer of shops available as well as independent mall traders, many of them living locally, who are encouraged to set up and run niche starter businesses with a view to progressing into larger premises.

The Centre remains a focal point of the local Northampton community, and has purposely fostered relationships and encouraged links with many of the local schools, theatre and stage schools as well as many other local community groups, giving them a public platform to promote their causes as well as the opportunity to perform within their own community.

Customer service is a major factor in the Centre's continued success, which in turn drives an increase in the number of visitors. Many special events have taken place in the past few years such as free music and entertainment for all ages, as well as investment in special effect lighting and Christmas decorations that one would normally expect to see in only the larger regional centres.

'Northampton Holdings' vision for the future includes further investment, expansion and development to ensure Weston Favell Shopping Centre continues to offer the best in shopping and remains at the heart of the Northampton community for many years to come.

Above: *Celebrating St George's Day in 2007.* ***Left.*** *Crowds having fun whilst being entertained at one of the Shopping Centre's many events.* ***Below:*** *Weston Favell's new extension.*

Michael Jones Jewellers

The Gold in Gold Street

Now with premises in Gold Street and the Grosvenor Centre, Northampton, and in the High Street, Banbury, Michael Jones Jewellers is a name to be reckoned with. But almost a century ago such prominence was still only a dream.

The year was 1919. The Great War had only recently ended and money was tight for a young Northampton couple Claude and Laurie Jones. The Joneses knew what they wanted from life, and that was to own their own business. With a rare determination they went ahead and took the plunge, sinking everything they had into the venture - including their wedding presents, which they sold to raise more capital.

Taking their remaining possessions with them – just a table, two chairs and a bed - they moved into number 45, Upper Mounts, where they lived above the shop.

The choice of goods they offered for sale, jewellery, drapery, clothing and a pawnbroker's service, reflected their backgrounds. Claude had been apprenticed to a pawnbroker in Marefair, Northampton, and had remained with the business until he had joined the army as an RAMC sergeant, serving in France where he carefully hoarded his modest pay for the business he intended to start.

Laurie had worked in a high class ladies' fashion shop until she, too, enlisted for war service.

The enterprising young couple set about establishing the business, providing a pawnbroking service, much appreciated by needy families in the area, and selling household goods, clothing and jewellery.

In 1923 they were able to employ their first shop assistant.

The years of worldwide economic depression between the wars were difficult and traumatic for Claude and Laurie - they found that their stock had lost half its value overnight. They faced up to the challenge, however, and survived. More difficulties followed during World War II, when owing to their business being classed as non-essential one of their two members of staff was called upon to be released for war work.

One of Claude and Laurie's sons, Michael, grew up to be as ambitious as his mother and father had been, and set about training in the Jewellery Quarters in Birmingham and Ipswich. In 1951, with National Service behind him, he joined his parents in the business. Over the next few years Michael improved the business, made alterations to the premises and employed younger staff.

When a property came up for sale next door but one in Upper Mounts, Michael bought it. Sadly, Claude did not live to see the move made by his son to concentrate entirely on jewellery and associated goods. Michael built a new shop on the nearby site he had bought, dedicated it to the sale of good class jewellery and watches, and named it Michael Jones Jeweller.

However, redevelopment in Northampton in the late 1960s forced the closure of the shops in Upper Mounts. A new town centre shop was opened at One Gold Street in 1970, where Michael Jones quickly established a reputation for quality. In the same year he turned the business into a co-operative - a step of which Michael is justifiably proud - and the business is now owned by its dedicated staff.

Still trading from the same address today, the business caters largely for those who want to give beautiful things to others (or to themselves!). Memorable gifts of choice gold jewellery with superior diamonds or coloured gemstones form part of the stock, along with a range of fine watches with such names as Rolex, Cartier, Tag Hueur, Omega, Gucci and Longines. Resident watchmakers and goldsmiths are there to give advice and service.

The company has come a long way since Claude and Laurie opened their first shop in 1919. Today's staff are fully trained and have gained appropriate qualifications including Fellowship of the Gemmological Society and Membership of the British Horological Institute.

As for the future, Michael Jones Jewellers and its Managing Director William Craghill, look forward to a continuing increase in the company's range and choice of merchandise, together with the ever-increasing expertise and qualifications of its staff - all with the aim of being recognised as the very best place to buy superior quality gifts that will remain forever special to those who receive them.

Facing page, top: *Claude Samuel Jones 1890-1960.* ***Facing page, bottom:*** *Michael Jones Jeweller - One Gold Street, Northampton.* ***Above:*** *William Craghill, Managing Director.* ***Below:*** *Michael Jones Jeweller - One Gold Street, Northampton, premises in 2011.*

T & K Precision - Committed to Excellence

T & K Precision is a family owned and run business established in 1961 and which is based in Northampton after relocating from London. It has become a specialist manufacturer to the Motor Racing Industry, producing high-tolerance, fast turnaround, Thread Rolled Studs and Fixings manufactured and completed, primarily for customers involved in the Formula One and Indy Cart Series. T & K operates from a 500sq. metre High Precision Production Plant on the Round Spinney Industrial Estate. The company also serves the Aerospace Industry, with many companies using T & K's thread rolling capabilities on complex components.

For the first twenty years, T & K Precision's work was MOD related, but as time went on others became aware of the quality of the work that the company routinely produced and the business expanded into the motor racing field where there was a need for high quality products.

T & K Precision's speciality is in the rolling of threads. The resulting features are a stronger component, since the material work hardens as it is formed, with a superior finish to that of a cut thread. Custom-made thread rolling machines are used to produce a wide range of precision threads for a variety of purposes.

The thread rolling process produces results far superior to those of traditional 'cut' threads, as the thread rolls used are optically ground and 'cold form' on to a pre-machined blank, producing a thread of perfect form, pitch and accuracy - within microns - whilst eliminating weak spots, stress points and the burrs and tool marks usually found on a cut thread.

Many GT Endurance and British Touring Car Teams are also being supplied exclusively by T & K Precision. Whole or part manufacture is available, with Turning/Grinding/Milling and other operations providing a complete service for all T & K's many national and international customers.

The highest standards in precision engineering is the company's main objective. It has therefore concentrated its capabilities on

Top left: *Co-founder Keith Forster and wife Yvonne.* ***Above:*** *The company's premises when built.* ***Below left:*** *A view of the Machine Shop in 1975.* ***Below:*** *Two of T & K Precision's Habeggar Swiss Plugboard machines bought in 1975. The one in the background was in service until 2010.*

the production of precision turned parts ranging in size from 3mm to 50mm diameter across a wide range of specialised materials, including nimonics (the generic name for a group of nickel-based heat-resistant alloys first developed in Britain in the early 1940s that typically contain chromium, titanium, and aluminium) and super alloys.

Its expertise in machining these materials to very close dimensional tolerances and surface finishes has won T & K many orders, not only from the motor racing industry, but also for applications such as Medical and Automotive equipment, Hydraulic and Pneumatic systems, Photographic and Audio-Visual equipment, as well as being a supplier to some national government installations.

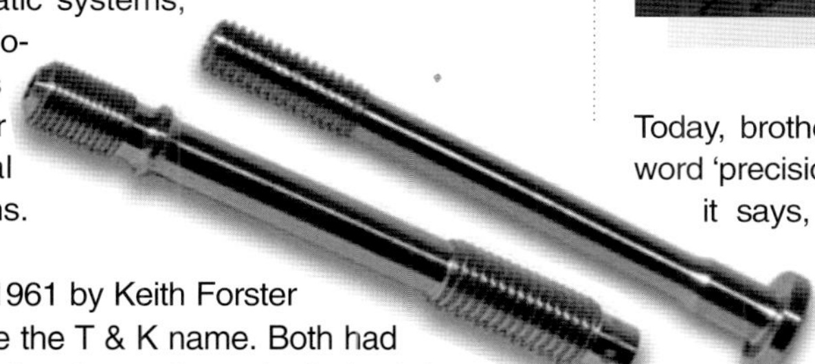

T & K was founded in 1961 by Keith Forster and Ted Penny – hence the T & K name. Both had previously worked in London, where both had been employed by Woodhills Engineering.

The pair started out in business on their own working from premises in Hervey Street, where they made stainless steel pistons and plastic seals using hand operated machinery.

The company moved to its present base at 10 Gatelodge Close, Round Spinney, in 1975 and it has subsequently also acquired number 9 Gatelodge Close, next door.

Specialised work initially came from Aerospace and defence contracts before the company began to offer its expertise to motor racing teams the world over.

The business became a 'family firm' in 1976 when Keith's son Clint joined the company, followed two years later by his brother Tim.

In the decades since it was founded T &K Precision Limited has established an unrivalled reputation for quality in the supply of the most accurate and precise products available today used not only in aircraft and racing cars, but also in boats.

The core business remains thread rolling, manufacturing complete parts or acting as a sub-contractor for thread rolled parts made by customers. T & K's CNC turning and grinding capability, along with conventional turning and milling, ensures it can offer the complete service. It can also provide parts complete with spark eroding, gun drilling, plating and heat treatments and titanium nitriding, all inspected to ISO 9002.

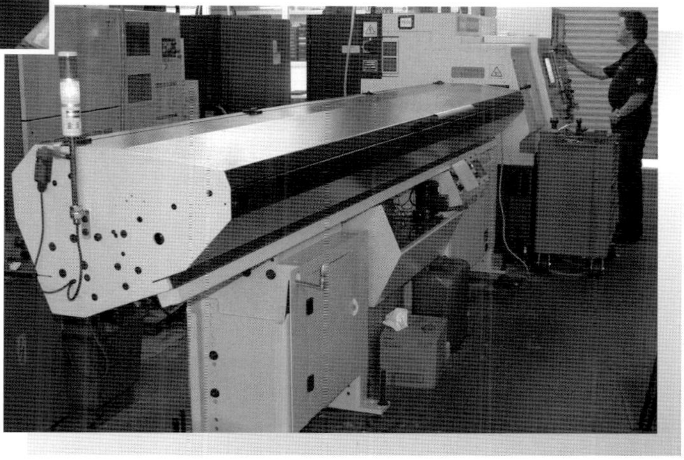

Today, brothers Clint and Tim Forster aim to ensure that the word 'precision' in the company title always means exactly what it says, with continual investment in the most modern equipment and machinery.

Top left and above: *T & K's latest asset – A Mazak Quickturn Nexus 100, with Hydrafeed hydraulic CNC barfeed, capable of feeding 5mm to 40mm bar diameter up to 3 metres long. Since the bar runs in oil, it can revolve at up to 6000 rpm without rattling about.This would be impossible with a traditional barfeed.* ***Centre:*** *An example of T & K Precision's rolled threads.* ***Below:*** *Two modern CNC bar fed machine tools.*

E. Gallone Ltd

Ice Cream and Sorbets Second to None, and a Service to Match

When Northampton's Giulio Gallone received a national award for making the best vanilla ice cream in Britain, it really was a case of having licked the rest!

The Gallone story goes back more than seventy years.

In 1930, Eduardo Gallone took his new wife, his childhood sweetheart Romelia, to start a new life. They boarded a boat to leave Italy bound for America. But they never made it; instead they got off the boat when it docked in Glasgow.

Eduardo was in fact no stranger to Britain; he had actually been born in Glasgow in 1910 the son of an ice cream merchant. His parents, however, had returned with him to their native Italy when Eduardo was just three years old.

Now at the age of 20 Eduardo was back in Scotland working for his sister and brother-in-law.

During the great Depression friends and family stayed in Scotland, but not Eduardo. He decided to head for the Midlands, to Northampton, where with his wife he began the business which would become E. Gallone Ltd.

The Gallones chose Northampton because at that time it was a boot and shoe manufacturing town and in their opinion, since people would always need shoes, there would be no unemployment.

In a small factory in Kingsthorpe, a little piece of Italy was kept alive in the form of an old family recipe for ice cream, one which happily proved to be immensely popular with the locals.

Italian ice-cream had long been a British favourite. An Italian businessman, Carlo Gatti, opened Britian's first ice cream stall outside London's Charing Cross station in 1851, selling scoops of ice cream for one penny. Italian ice cream salesmen, the famous 'Hokey-pokey' men riding tricycles with insulated cold boxes, were once a familiar sight. Still-familiar terms such as a Tutti-fruti and a '99' both have their origins in Italy.

In Northampton, fresh milk arrived daily, delivered in churns from Brampton Dairies in Castilian Street. Ice cream and other provisions were sent out in a horse and cart. The Gallone name became well known and children would run out to the vans carrying bowls to be filled.

The little factory was soon too small and in 1938 a move was made to Trinity Avenue. By then the Gallones were operating three ice cream vans.

Top: *Eduardo and Romelia Gallone.* ***Left and above:*** *There's was always a queue for a Gallone's ice cream as these scenes from the early years show.*

Trinity Avenue was to be home to the factory throughout the war. Yet the rationing of ingredients and fuel for some time meant that ice cream was designated a luxury and could no longer be manufactured.

Eduardo was unfit for military service but instead went to work in a factory in Rugby; he also became a part-time ambulance driver.

When restrictions were lifted after the war Eduardo resumed his ice cream business, supplying a generation of delighted children who had grown up in the war rarely seeing sweets or tasting ice cream

The next decade brought another move. In 1949 the firm transferred to Welford Road where the firm is still based. The Gallone family in the meantime had grown, with a son Giulio and a daughter, Romelia. In the late 1950s they both joined the family business.

As the 1960s dawned, the new generation of Gallones started to take the helm, Guilio and Romelia began to run the factory alongside their parents. In 1963 two big ice cream families were united by the marriage of Giulio to Dorina Di Mascio from Di Di's, of Coventry.

But it was not all good news. That same year, 1963, half the Welford Road site was compulsory purchased and the factory had to be re-built.

Yet, undeterred, the company now went from strength to strength, developing new flavours and increasing the range, yet always keeping to the strict quality of the old family recipe.

As the company has grown so has the family. Giulio and Dorina's sons, Aldo and Lorenzo are now taking the helm. After four decades Giulio, Dorina and Romelia can step back, knowing that the children have grown up with Gallone's ice cream. They still share the same passion for good, quality ice cream, produced in the old family way, whilst expanding into the wholesale market which today has become a major part of the business.

Above left: *Another large queue at a Gallone ice cream van in the 1960s.* ***Below left:*** *The Di Mascio fleet in the 1960s.* ***Above:*** *Giulio Gallone receiving the National Award, 'Best in Britain' for Vanilla Ice Cream in 2000.* ***Below:*** *E Gallone Ltd's Welford Road premises.*

Sheinman Opticians - Clear Vision for the Future in Eyecare and Eyewear

AE Turville OBE to JS Sheinman

Albert Edward Turville's interest in spectacles and eye problems began towards the end of the 19th century when, as a small boy, he would help his father, a Northampton watchmaker and jeweller. Pairs of spectacles were often handed in to the shop for repair, which encouraged the young Albert Edward to take an interest. He had eye problems of his own, and the myopic astigmatism he suffered from fostered his interest in ophthalmic optics. He went on to pass the British Optical Association examination in 1914 and the following year saw him set up a practice in premises that had once housed a doctor's surgery in Abington Street, Northampton. He made his home on the premises, and the consulting room during the day was his sitting room outside working hours.

It was from there that the enthusiastic young ophthalmic optician began to carry out his many research projects. His special interest was in the practical area of instrument design and construction, and over the next 45 years he was to develop many outstanding clinical systems and innovative optical instruments including, in 1927, the prototype for the renowned Turville-Stewart ophthalmoscope, hand slit lamp and retinoscope. Turville's publications were many and varied, from papers on his research into sight testing techniques and binocular vision correction to treatments for the partially sighted and migraine sufferers.

A leading figure in the British optical world, Mr Turville became advisor to the government during the establishment of the NHS.

His expertise and comprehensive knowledge of his subject gathered over many years combined to earn him a worldwide reputation in the field. In recognition of his activities he was awarded an OBE and he received a number of honorary fellowships for his work internationally. Outside the workplace, Mr Turville had many interests. He was an amateur radio ham in the years before the Second World War, which led to an involvement with the Foreign Service Broadcasting – espionage activities before and during the war!

A key decision was taken in 1964 when John Sheinman joined Mr Turville in the practice. Sadly, AE Turville died only a year later and John was left to carry on alone. Building on his predecessor's reputation, John Sheinman proceeded to develop this remarkable practice into one of the foremost centres for eye care in Europe. 1982-1995 saw a period of intense expansion into the adjoining buildings on either side. Today, the practice covers an amazing 10,000 square feet. It is considered to be the largest optometric practice in Europe and

Top: *Albert Edward Turville, the founder of the Practice.* ***Below left:*** *A E Turville's 1930s consulting room makes an interesting comparison to the state-of-the-art facilities as found in the Practice today.* ***Below:*** *John Sheinman.*

the research and development of clinical equipment remains an important part of their work. The vast majority of Sheinman patients come from Northamptonshire, with around five percent living outside the county. The first impression on entering the building is of an extensive and well-designed operation. The theme of dispensing and the sight testing areas are developed quite separately as in the past, but very naturally blend into a single inter-dependent unit.

The environment differs from that of most high street practices due to the spacious and relaxed atmosphere. Research rooms on the premises provide the necessary space for ongoing study and investigation, while the firm's optical laboratory was significantly enlarged in recent years to embrace every modern concept of spectacle design and manufacture.

Sheinman Opticians provide an exciting and comprehensive choice of frames in a vast showroom, benefiting from natural daylight from an atrium roof. Much admired is their unique video system 'Eye TV' allowing patients to try on frames and then compare options on screen – an innovative way of choosing the right pair of spectacles. In addition they employ computer programmes that show how current lens technology relates to the patient's own particular needs, also providing a price guide as a useful reference.

And the future.....

Sheinman Opticians' programme of ongoing expansion and research will continue to closely involve children's eyecare – an area of study that interestingly had been of particular significance to AE Turville back in the late 1920s. Projects as diverse as computerised online sight testing systems, exclusive eyewear design and preserving the sight of the ageing eye also remains at the hub of their activities.

Since Mr Turville set up the practice in 1915, genuine patient care and the ability to offer a more fully comprehensive eyecare service than average has been the key to the success of this unique practice. Their aim is to continually explore new and even better ways to provide the most advanced total eyecare for their patients and customers as they enter their second 100 years of service in Northampton.

***Above** The front of the Practice until 1975 - the last 'house' in Abington Street. **Below:** The entrance reception. **Bottom:** View of the Practice on Abington Street from 1996 prior to major changes due in 2012.*

A Bell & Co Ltd - The Home of Good Design

The showrooms of A Bell & Company, in Kingsthorpe Road, Kingsthorpe, feature a wonderful selection of top quality kitchens, bathrooms, heating appliances and fireplaces. Yet it was back in the 19th century, in 1898, that Ablett Bell opened his ironmongers shop in Gold Street.

Two years later Ablett was joined by brothers Frank and Harry Jelley. As well as ironmongery the partnership would soon sell kitchen ranges and a new type of open fire: the company's famous Canopy Dog Grates.

By 1905 the firm had expanded into a four-storey warehouse in Kingswell Street. In 1908, when the firm became a limited company, it achieved international recognition gaining four gold medals and the Grand Prix for its grates at the Franco-English exhibition. Around this time, tile interiors and kerbs began to be produced at Kingswell Street, as well as tiled surrounds. Local sales calls would be made by bicycle, whilst visits to far flung places, such as Rugby and Wolverton, would require the traveller to take the train. Local orders were taken by horse-drawn transport and hand carts.

Bell's first catalogue included Bell's own cooking ranges and fires, gas lighting, coal-fired coppers, boilers and heating stoves, WCs, wash basins and baths, cisterns, stable stalls and harness room fittings along with a large section of ironmongery.

Early heating appliances were mostly designed for solid fuel which called for a very flexible method of installation: a tinsmith made special fittings for each individual job. A long remembered item is the Combination Grate which had an open fire combined with one or two ovens, and sometimes a fireback boiler. Engraving plates for coffins was another area of business; they were supplied to country builders who sometimes doubled up as

undertakers. After engraving, the brass plates would be despatched by bus, parceled up with a lining shroud and wadding.

By 1927, the year of Ablett Bell's death, the firm had a showroom in the West End of London whilst a new production site had been built on a three acre site on the Thornton Estate at Kingsthorpe.

A Bell & Co felt the impact of war, quite literally, when in July 1941 a Stirling bomber crashed on top of the Gold Street premises. The shop front and a great deal of stock were destroyed. It took until September to clear the shop area of debris.

Top left: *Company founder Mr Ablett Bell.* ***Top right:*** *Mr Bell's premises in the early 1900s.* ***Left:*** *The showroom and offices on Gold Street, 1909.* ***Above:*** *The factory premises at Kingsthorpe, built in 1926.*

The firm's London showroom was destroyed, never to reopen. At Kingsthorpe, production was switched to the making of pre-cast concrete air raid shelters and paraffin lamps. By 1943 all the factory space was being used as stores for the US Army. The iron railings around the factory were removed as salvage to help the war effort and were replaced by ornate concrete wall capping, some of which can still be seen.

Following the war, Bell's range of products increased to include cutlery, pewter and silverware, vases, fenders, trays and mirrors.

The old Majestic Cinema, in Gold Street, was bought and rebuilt in 1952 so that both showrooms could be housed together, warehouse goods being transferred to Horseshoe Street opposite.

In 1956, Bell's became a Calor Gas dealer which would lead to the firm becoming the region's major supplier of Calor Gas and equipment.

Since the early 1980s the company has also been a distributor for the famed Aga cooker.

In 1984, the last link with Gold Street was severed when the whole business was moved to Kingsthorpe Road. The redeveloped premises feature a massive showroom of some 13,000 sq. ft. containing the leading Kitchen Design Studio in the area, a vast range of Bathroom equipment, and an outstanding Tile Centre, alongside one of the largest displays of Fireplaces and heating appliances in the country. Adjoining the main showroom is a specialist Calor Gas Centre.

The company remained jointly owned by the Bell and Jelley families until July 2005, when under the leadership of the Managing Director John Kirkham, a management buy-out took place with the full support of the founding families, who still retain a small shareholding.

In recent years the company has won a number of accolades including the 'Retailer of the Year Award' presented by the Northamptonshire Business Excellence Awards. The judges commented: "A customer survey shows how dedicated it is to both its business and its customers. The presentation of its showroom and literature is of a very high standard, which inspires confidence in its products from a customer's point of view."

Today, with its extensive premises and huge range of products from leading brands such as Aga Cookers, Clearview Stoves, Siematic Kitchens, Miele Appliances, Villeroy Boch Bathrooms and Hans Grohe Showers, Bell's offers visitors the kind of welcome which Ablett Bell would have been most proud of.

Top left: *A police officer at the scene of devastation following the Stirling Bomber crash in 1941.* ***Above:*** *An Aga cooker circa 1935.* ***Below:*** *The firm's current premises on Kingsthorpe Road, Northampton.*

Dickens Brothers Ltd - Going Well for Leather

Dickens Brothers Ltd based in Kettering Road, Northampton, is one of the oldest established leather manufacturers and merchants in the UK.

The firm's speciality is vegetable-tanned kipsides and cowcalf leather. With unequalled experience in providing leather for a vast range of uses, about half of the company's output is exported.

Dickens Brothers Ltd is a small family company, which has been producing leather since 1897. The founder of Dickens Brothers, William John Dickens, was born in 1860, the son of a village shoemaker.

John Dickens (his preferred choice of name) spent all of his early working years in various leather-related trades before deciding to set up his own business. Two years after starting out on his own, in 1899, he decided that new premises were necessary and acquired land to have a purpose-built factory constructed in Kettering Road, Northampton. This was completed in 1900 and this is where the company he founded still produces leather to this day.

At his new factory John Dickens produced hand stuffed or curried English vegetable tanned calfskins and cowhides, black or tan in colour. The 'stuffing' mixture was cod oil and tallow, with lamp black for the black coloured leather. The finished product was good quality boot leather.

Sadly, John Dickens did not live long enough to see his firm flourish. He died in 1903 at the age of just 43. His eldest sons, Alfred and Arnold, then aged just 20 and 18, were left to run the business.

In 1906 the firm started buying hides from Madras in India.

Arnold would travel by train selling the firm's products. In 1908 he went on a selling trip to the USA starting a long standing export trade to America and Canada.

A younger brother, Reginald, was by now also in the business, but in 1914 he joined the army, rising to the rank of Captain in the Machine Gun Corps. The firm played its bit by supplying leather for army boots.

Reginald rejoined his brothers in 1919 in time for the firm of J Dickens to be incorporated as Dickens Brothers Ltd in 1921.

The export trade continued to grow, with Alfred travelling extensively in Europe in search of orders.

Reginald left the company in 1934 to establish his own firm.

Top left: *Founder, William John Dickens.* ***Left:*** *Employees at Victoria Street in 1898.* ***Top right:*** *Alfred Dickens.* ***Centre page:*** *Arnold Dickens.* ***Above:*** *Reginald and Bernard Dickens.*

For Dickens Brothers business continued uninterrupted until the Second World War. Shortage of imported raw materials now meant the firm using horse shanks, donkey, badger, deer skins and even dog skins. Leather for special flying boots for the RAF came from the firm – the upper parts of the boots could be removed, enabling shot down airmen to pass as civilians.

The youngest Dickens brother, Bernard, had joined the firm before the Second World War. In 1946, he persuaded his brothers to buy an existing factory in Pine Street, trading as 'Impress'. Now it used off-cuts from Dickens Brothers to make into heel lifts. The factory was, however, sold when Bernard left the firm in 1957, which he did when both Alfred and Reginald died that year and he was needed to take over Reginald's business interests.

Meanwhile the next generation had already joined the family business.

Alfred's son, Stephen, joined in 1947. A year later he was followed by his younger brother, Richard.

Arnold's son, Brian, joined the company in 1959.

In 1980, the company ceased dressing leather at Kettering Road. Production however, continued much as before, with hides still imported, though now from Sri Lanka rather than India.

Stephen retired in 1994 leaving Brian to take the company through to its centenary in 1997.

During a century which saw many industrial disputes in the wider economy, Dickens Brothers was hardly affected. In fact, in the general strike of 1926 just a handful of days were lost. Good working relations have always been important. At least ten Dickens Brothers' employees have clocked up more than 50 years' service during its existence. The spirit of the company has always been that the directors worked alongside the employees, and today Brian Dickens can be seen in the warehouse amongst bales of rough leather and 'horses' of finished leather.

Despite the passage of time Dickens Brothers Ltd remains that rare thing, a real family firm still committed to producing a very real product – leather.

Top left and top right: *Views inside Dickens Brothers Ltd in 1929.* ***Bottom left:*** *From left to right: Richard Dickens, Stephen Dickens and Brian Dickens.* ***Left:*** *Dickens Brothers Ltd's Kettering Road premises.* ***Below:*** *At work inside Dickens Brothers Ltd in 2012.*

Springline Ltd - The Last People

Springline is the only last company in the UK still manufacturing bulk lasts. Most of the older generation will know what a last is – but for those who do not, a last is the inside form of the shoe, the shoe being constructed around the last. The last not only gives the shoe its shape, but also it's fitting qualities.

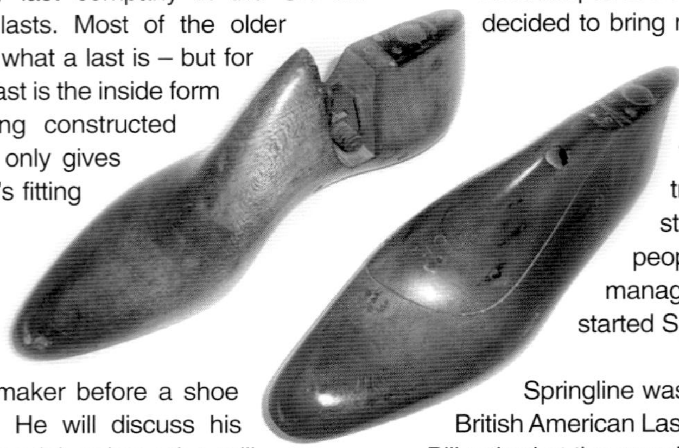

The last comes first, and maybe should have been called a 'first' instead of 'last' as it is required by the shoemaker before a shoe designer can start his work. He will discuss his requirements with the last model-maker who will interpret his instructions into the last in order to produce the type of shoe required.

Back in the 1960s all the lasts were made from Canadian maple wood - this becoming harder to obtain over the years has meant that bulk production has had to change to plastic high density polyethylene (HDPE). O.A.Miller was the first to produce plastic lasts in 1962. They are are a lot heavier than wood but more durable. The only wooden lasts manufactured today are for the bespoke trade (made-to-measure).These are made out of hornbeam or beech.

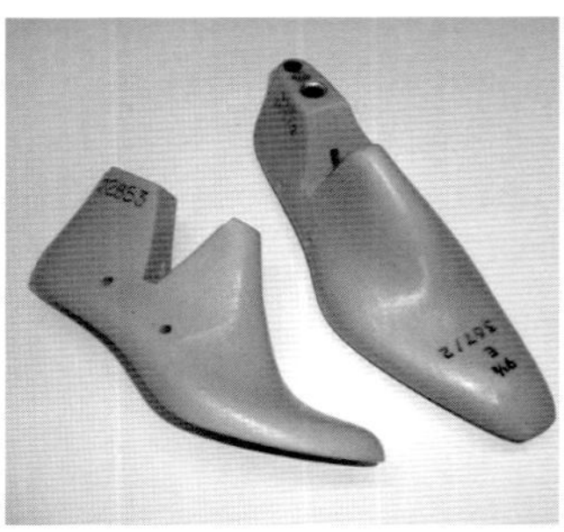

Springline was formed in November 1982 by Ken Tipping and Bill Saunders.

Ken and Bill started their careers at the British American Last Works in St Michael's Road, Northampton. Ken joined the Company in January 1962 straight from school, aged 15. Bill had started a year earlier.

Mobbs Miller 'Kettering' who were the largest and strongest competitors brought British American in 1980 and closed the factory down making everyone redundant.

At this time British footwear manufacturing was in huge decline with large factories closing every month.

A two year spell of trying to import lasts from Italy under the name 'Style Team' in Desborough under the umbrella of R.S. Lawrence followed. However, that did not work out due to late deliveries and the poor quality of Italian lasts which Northamptonshire factories could not work with. The pair decided to bring manufacturing back to the UK – despite that being a big risk.

Happily, it was at the time Margaret Thatcher was Prime Minister and was trying to encourage new businesses to start up by offering unsecured loans to people not already in business. Ken and Bill managed to secure one of those loans and started Springline in 1982.

Springline was formed with two other ex-employees of British American Last Company - Bill Baxter and Keith Harris, Bill retired at the grand age of 79 and Keith still works part time and is 70 this year.

Above: *Old wooden lasts.* ***Below left:*** *New plastic lasts.* ***Below:*** *Model makers at work.*

The Company started trading in Pondwood Close, Moulton Park Industrial Estate, Northampton, and in 1989 moved to larger premises next door, which it still occupies, now employing 24 people.

Springline became Britain's only last makers in 2002 when Mobbs Miller closed down.

Michael James joined Springline in 1984, shortly after leaving school, and followed in the footsteps of Ken and Bill – learning the technical skills by working his way through the factory. Michael has proved to be a big asset to the Company and was eventually made a director/shareholder. He now looks after sales and overseeing the model room creating all new developments for all of the major footwear brands based in the UK.

In the early year's shoe lasts were Springline's only product, but with repeated recessions most of the ladies' and children's footwear was lost, with factories closing down due to cheap imports. With the loss of these customers the business had to change.

It now manufactures high quality shoe fillers/trees. These are sold with the shoes to maintain their quality whilst not being worn. Shoe trees now represent half of all production.

Another area which has increased significantly over the years is 'bespoke', where individual customers have their own lasts made to their exact foot measurements.

Clients for which Springline has made bespoke lasts for include the Queen mother, the 7th Duke of Wellington, Sir Paul McCartney and Sir Paul Smith, to name but a few.

Springline has also expanded on point of sale items for high street brands to display in shop windows from wooden heads to cloven hoofs.

Major changes in last manufacturing have come about because Springline now use CAD (computer-aided design). The firm can also make changes to the last on the computer which in the past would have been done by hand. Last data can also now be imported and exported via the internet.

Northampton continues to be strong in footwear manufacture, having managed to survive periodic recessions by continuing to make high-quality men's Goodyear-welted footwear which is appreciated worldwide. Springline is proud to be part of that success.

The future looks promising and the shoe industry will certainly never see the last of lasts!

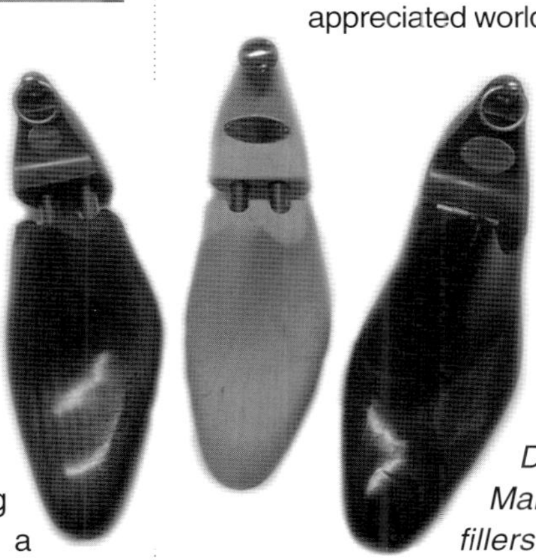

Top left: *Michael James, Sales Director (left) and Ken Tipping, Managing Director.* ***Left:*** *Quality shoe fillers.* ***Below:*** *The Springline factory pictured in February 2009.*

C. Butt Ltd - Going the Extra Mile

Today, C. Butt Ltd is one of the region's best known transport, warehousing and 'logistics' providers.

Company founder, Charles Butt, left the forces in 1919 and bought 12 acres of land in Weedon Road which he used for market gardening and rearing pigs.

Having a horse and cart he was able to undertake casual haulage work for the council, and his fledgling transport business soon prospered.

In 1926 Charles was joined by his nephew, William 'Bill' Butt. Before long their first tipper lorry was acquired.

Larger vehicles and a property at Stenson Street followed. Regular runs were being made to London, Liverpool and Bristol for local mills, contractors, builders and breweries. Often return loads were off-loaded at Stenson Street and vehicles reloaded for the next day. Local work continued to be important: deliveries for allotment holders and stall holders at Northampton market, as well as carrying sand and gravel from local sandpits.

With an increasing workload, Weedon Road Garage, where vehicle maintenance took place, was acquired and was where Cyril Starr was recruited in 1946.

During the Second Word War some of the vehicles had to be allocated to work for the Ministry of War. By the end of the war 22 vehicles were being operated, with drivers' wages in 1946 being just 75 shillings (£3 75p) for a 48 hour week.

Manager Tom Crouch died in 1947 and was succeeded by his assistant Cyril Starr.

In 1948 the Labour Government nationalised road transport and C & WH Butt was taken over by British Road Services. In protest Cyril Starr left the firm. Cyril Starr joined Bill Butt working at the Weedon Road garage under the name of A Butt, a separate firm operating three tipper lorries and licensed to work only within a 25-mile radius.

Other small local firms were soon bought out by A Butt giving the new

Top left: *W.H Butt (the Guv'nor) a founder of the company.* ***Above:*** *The first brand new diesel engined vehicle purchased by Butts; a 1947 ERF 54G.* ***Below:*** *1959 Scammell Highwayman 25 tons low loader.*

business 14 vehicles, each with separate licensing restrictions. An arrangement with Mackay Transport Ltd, of Watford, soon allowed A Butt to recommence long distance haulage work.

In 1953 several tippers had to be allocated for work on sea defence repair caused by the East coast floods. Butt lorries carried slag from Scunthorpe and Immingham to the disaster areas.

When de-nationalisation began in 1952 Charles and Bill Butt were able to buy back a number of vehicles from BRS - all licensed to travel to any part of Britain.

New workshops, offices and a lorry park were erected in Spencer Bridge Road in 1954. The following year C. Butt Ltd was created, the shareholders being Charles Butt, William H Butt and Cyril Starr.

Brian Butt joined C. Butt Ltd on completion of National Service in 1956 and was soon working for ST Challis Ltd, a cattle haulage company based in Badby bought by Butts in 1952. In the years that followed acquisition would follow acquisition.

More members of the family joined the firm, Gerald Butt in 1960 - now the company Chairman - followed by John Butt, and then by their sons, Robert and Jonathon in the 1980s. Clive Hodgkinson joined the company in 1983 as General Manager.

Butt vehicles continued to haul building materials for many local landmarks including the M1 motorway, the second cooling tower (now gone) at Northampton Power Station and the Express Lift Tower.

Charles Butt, the firm's founder, passed away in 1980. Cyril Starr retired in 1983. In the 1980s and 90s the company continued to expand, winning several industry awards and opening depots in Corby, Wellingborough, Middlewich and Wakefield, and now operating in excess of 200 vehicles.

In 2000 this award-winning firm acquired more premises on the Lodge Farm Industrial estate where in 2003 a new bespoke headquarters was constructed.

Three years later Hyundai and C. Butt Solutions Ltd ('Global 2 Local') was created as a joint venture company.

The opening of a centralised 'control tower' in 2011 to develop transport networking underlined C. Butt's on-going commitment to 'always going the extra mile'.

Above left: *The world's first ERF 8 wheeler to be powered by a Cummins diesel engine, first registered in 1962.* ***Top right:*** *The board of directors celebrating the 50th anniversary of C. Butt Ltd. Pictured are (from left to right), W.R.Butt (Director), C.Starr (Joint MD), W.H.Butt (Chairman), C.Butt (Vice Chairman), G.W.Butt (Joint MD), J.Butt (Director), B.Butt (Director).* ***Below:*** *C. Butt Ltd's new livery.*

Richard Finch & Sons - A Final Service

The firm of Richard Finch & Sons independent family funeral directors came into being in 1965, created by the husband and wife team of Richard F.J. Finch and Nora I. Finch. The '& Sons' in the name was a later addition. The firm moved to its current premises at 77, Military Road in 1970. Since then it has become the largest funeral home in Northampton.

With its own 20-space car park, and Northampton's only dedicated remembrance room, the funeral home features a book which contains the names of every funeral conducted by the firm since it began.

Today, the firm runs a brand new fleet of Jaguar Hearse and Limousines, helping providing bereaved families in Northampton with the very best quality of service.

Every funeral is directed by the current partners, the '& Sons', brothers Richard Jnr and Adam Finch, each dedicated to giving families the best possible personal attention.

The Finch family will help deal with every aspect of a bereavement, including flowers, service sheets and insertion in the local newspapers. Catering at their own private premises and memorials are also available. Help and advice is also given for probate and social fund.

After suffering a bereavement, a funeral for a member of ones family can be the most difficult day of one's life. Everything family and friends ever thought about a loved one is expressed on that day.

As funeral directors Richard Finch & Sons is there to help and advise in whatever way they can. They are dedicated professionals who provide a personal service 24 hours a day, 365 days a year.

The firm's premises have been constantly improved to provide families with the best possible funeral home, including a spacious reception area for families to reflect while paying their last respects to their loved ones.

Brothers, Richard and Adam Finch, the founders' two sons, conduct every funeral personally. No matter what type of funeral is being conducted the family of funeral directors gives the same detailed care and attention to each and every one.

Company founders Richard F. J. Finch and Nora I. Finch began their business life in the private car hire business in 1952. On 1 September, 1965,

Top:** Founders, Richard and Nora Finch.* ***Above and left: *Part of the Richard Finch & Sons fleet of Jaguar Hearse and Limousines.*

however, they started their funeral business in Victoria Street, Northampton, before moving to their present premises in Military Road.

During the 1970s and 80s the Finch family built up a loyal clientele, and not just within the funeral business; they also serviced weddings and long distance private hire.

Meanwhile, their funeral home was constantly updated to providethe very best facilities in Northampton for the benefit of the deceased and their loved ones. They completed an extension to the premises in 1992 to include a dedicated remembrance room.

Business founder Richard passed away in 2007, whilst Nora continued in the firm until she passed away suddenly in 2009.

Their sons Richard and Adam now continue the family tradition.

Richard was born in Northampton in 1958. He was educated at Weston Favell before joining the family business in 1974. He directs all funerals himself. With nearly four decades of experience within the business he is an expert in all aspects of embalming, and oversees every aspects of paying last respects. He prides himself on being a perfectionist. Richard still lives locally at Millwood Park.

Born in Wootton in 1966, Adam Finch was educated at Northampton School for Boys then joined the family firm in 1982. Working very closely with his father, he learned all the aspects of the funeral business. Now with some 30 years at the Military Road funeral home behind him he still attends all the 'first-call' meetings with families and with nursing homes. He believes it is essential to keep a personal contact with families from start to finish. Adam now lives in the village of Overstone.

According to Richard and Adam "It is a rare privilege to be a funeral director, to stand in a sensitive position at a crucial time in the midst of a family, knowing that the quality of one's service and reputation will help them through one of the most difficult time in their lives."

***Top and above left:** Richard Finch & Sons' Military Road premises and spacious reception area. **Below:** Richard (left) and Adam Finch.*

Wardle & Keach - A Moving Story

Wardle & Keach International Ltd, based at Clifford Hill, Little Houghton, is the area's largest independent removal and storage company. The firm was formed in 1926 by the amalgamation of two family businesses, one of which had roots going back to 1890.

Albert Wardle came from the village of Kegworth to manage Liptons in Kettering. In 1900, at the age of forty, he went into partnership with a Mr Jacques, an already established coal haulier, who died a few years later. Messrs A Wardle and Son, founded in 1905, continued the coal haulage business. Harold Wardle took over from his father and ran the business into the 1920s. Meanwhile, George Keach, from Melton Ernest, in Bedfordshire, had also migrated to Kettering. He, too, delivered coal from horse-drawn vehicles before progressing to general haulage in 1912 when he bought some steam traction engines. In time the business passed to his son Charles who ran it as a sole trader. The two firms worked side by side, more often in co-operation than in competition, until, in 1926, the two young men

decided that they would benefit by amalgamating. Wardle & Keach operated from the Keach premises in Crown Street where they worked hard to expand the coal business, and also to develop a furniture removal enterprise until the outbreak of war in 1939. In the war years some of the firm's vital lorries were commandeered for war use and Harold Wardle's son, Norman, was conscripted into the RAF. On Norman Wardle's return in 1946 he found things rather run-down, and the patched-up vehicles running on cannibalised parts, like so many around the country, were literally on their last wheels. In 1947 Charles Keach's nephew, a Mr Panter, joined Norman in rebuilding the

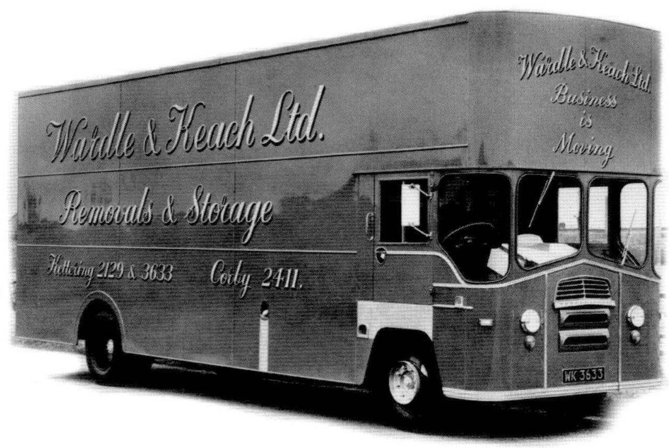

war-weary company. Their priority was to obtain new lorries, firstly furniture vans to take war evacuees back to their homes in bomb-battered London, then coal lorries. Wardle and Keach supplied 90% of all Kettering factories with coal, plus all the

***Top:** George Keach's removal van at Wollaston in the early years. **Left:** Loading up at Stamford Road, Kettering. **Above:** An early Thames Trader van.*

schools in Kettering, Corby and all the surrounding villages with their coal rations. The firm collected coal from the nearby collieries, setting up a coal depot on a plot of land bought for that purpose. The furniture side of the business was also expanding and needed storage space, so an empty factory was bought and converted for use as a furniture repository. The influx of American service families joining airmen stationed at USAF bases at Grafton Underwood, Molesworth and Mildenhall meant that up to ten 6-12 ton loads of crated furniture and possessions were arriving daily: a fork lift truck was purchased to load and unload the crates. The firm also entered the export business for the USAF.

Norman Wardle retired in 1985. His son Peter ran the company briefly but then decided to sell to another local firm, Henry's Removals. Paul and Sue Henry became the new owners of Wardle & Keach in 1986, keeping Peter on as company accountant and moving the business to their existing premises

in Kingswell Street. A larger site was soon required, however, and in 1988 the firm moved to purpose-built warehouse premises on the Brixworth Industrial Estate.

The company's current site at Little Houghton was bought in 1991, and construction of a new warehouse was completed in 1993. Wardle & Keach's growth continued through acquisition: Frosts Removals in 1987, William Olivers in 1991, Hillyards Removals in 1998, Pittham Removals in 2007 and are currently in negotiation for a further limited company, hoping to finalise in early 2012. Today, a fleet of vehicles with expert crews carries out local, national and international removals, and another warehouse has been constructed providing 10,000 square feet of containerised storage, whilst the original warehouse is now used for archive storage, extending the firm's commercial and office removals service.

Paul and Sue Henry's daughter, Hannah, performed various tasks such as packing duties and acting as office junior before going on to obtain a degree in Business Studies and becoming the firm's Corporate Accounts and Liaison Officer. Son James joined the company on a full-time basis in 2006 as a porter and like his sister Hannah has worked his way up through the firm, learning packing/loading and export packing skills. In addition to this he successfully gained his Counterbalance and Reach Truck licences and at the age of 21 acquired his LGV2 licence

enabling him to drive the firms largest Rigid 17 ton vehicles. In 2011 he was appointed Warehouse Manager and became responsible for the efficient administration of both containerised storage and archive movements. Heavy investment has gone into the specialised aspect of document management and to this end state-of-the-art equipment has been installed to enable the smooth running of all document/data movements – giving customers the opportunity of being able to view for themselves their documents on the World Wide Web.

2011 was an extremely good year for Wardle & Keach and at the end of that year they purchased a brand new 17 ton pantechnicon which will be sign written supporting the local Saints Rugby Club with whom the company has had a special affinity for a number of years.

In becoming the largest independent removal company in the area, Wardle & Keach has remained throughout a family-run concern with a caring attitude and a commitment to quality - twin values which have brought success during the 20th century and will continue to do so in the 21st.

Above left: *The company was commissioned to move restored pictures from Althorp in the late 1980s.* ***Top right:*** *A near disaster above the M4. The motorway was closed to clear the stricken van.* ***Below:*** *Wardle & Keach moved a customer into The Manor House in Great Addington and also, in 2011, relocated them from there as seen below.*

Cosworth - A Winning Partnership

It is now more than half a century since Mike Costin and Keith Duckworth decided to go into partnership, combining their surnames and talents to create what was to become famed as Cosworth.

Since its formation, Cosworth has become a leading provider of high performance technologies in a diverse range of industries including Aerospace, Defence, Automotive and competitive Sport.

Despite the two founders having now retired, the legendary name of Cosworth still remains respected throughout the world: the company was named UK Manufacturer of the Year 2011.

Founded in 1958, Cosworth first operated from premises at Edmonton, in London. According to Keith Duckworth the pair thought it must be possible to make an 'interesting living messing about with racing cars and engines'. Neither of them envisaged the world-wide reputation they would eventually acquire. In their first year, turnover amounted to just £3,666 and the business made a loss.

By 1963, when the business moved to St James Mill Road, in Northampton, turnover had reached almost £100,000. Neither of the two partners had ever been to Northampton, but decided that it was an ideal location close to the newly constructed M1 motorway and a new factory was built for £8,000. It was a wise move.

In 1966, Duckworth signed a contract with Ford to develop a new three-litre Formula One engine, and the legendary Cosworth DFV was born. It got its first taste of victory in its very first race, when in 1967 Jim Clark took the chequered flag in his Lotus 49 at the Dutch Grand Prix. The DFV went on to dominate the sport for 15 years and clinched 155 race wins. During this period Cosworth engines also crossed the Atlantic to take the Indy/CART world by storm. Here, the DFX version of the F1 powerplant took an incredible 151 race wins in a 14-year reign, including ten drivers' championships and ten Indianapolis 500 victories.

***Top left:** Keith Duckworth and Mike Costin, company founders. **Above:** Cosworth was built up in the late 1960s by four directors, left to right: Bill Brown, Keith Duckworth, Mike Costin and Ben Rood. **Left:** Victory first time out. Jim Clark drove the Ford DFV-engined Lotus 49 to victory in its maiden race, the Dutch F1 Grand Prix in June 1967.*

As the 1980s became the 90s, Cosworth continued to provide winning power, with the Ford Sierra Cosworth RS500 taking the 1987 Touring Car world title and the Cosworth-powered Ford Mondeo winning the World titles in 1993 and 1994.

In Formula One, the DFV won 11 races between 1989 and 1993, and this was in turn superceded by in 1994 by the Zetec V8 F1 engine which powered Michael Schumacher's first world driver's title.

The XB engine burst onto the Indy car scene in 1992 and was the foundation for a family of engines which are still in use today. The XB was a success both on and off the track, and sales led to Cosworth being awarded the Queen's Award for Export Achievement.

In rallying, the Ford Escort RS Cosworth notched up numerous wins during the 1990s and the Duratec-R engine in the Focus WRC gave Ford more success.

A partnership was formed with Opel in the mid 1990s which culminated in winning the DTM International Touring Car Championship in 2006.

That same period witnessed the spectacular growth of motorsport electronics and the establishment of data recording and analysis as a cornerstone of motorsport. Cosworth's Pi Research on-car data acquisition systems were some of the first electronic dash display and data loggers to be used in professional motor sport.

Cosworth and Pi Research were bought by Ford in 1998. A year later the acquisition of Pectel Control Systems as a division of Pi Research extended its range of electronics expertise and technologies to include engine controllers. A new facility in Mooresville, NC (USA), was also opened in 1999.

Success continued in the wider business arena, and in 2003 Cosworth was voted the MIA business of the year.

The Ford era ended in 2004 when Cosworth and and Pi Research were sold by Ford, and the Cosworth Group of companies was formed.

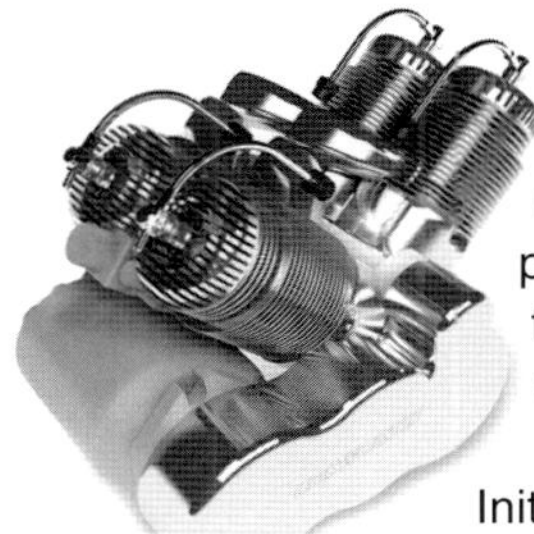

The formation of the Cosworth Group began a diversification program to develop new opportunities for the technologies that had delivered such success in motorsport.

Initial interest in the aerospace sector centred around flight test instrumentation and Cosworth's extensive array of precision manufacturing capabilities.

That diversification program has accelerated, and today the technologies which established Cosworth in the world of motorsport have provided the foundation for Cosworth as a global provider of advanced technological solutions.

Top left: *Another CA engine nearing completion.* ***Top right:*** *Cosworth acquires IP for lightweight heavy fuel engines.* ***Above left and above:*** *Cosworth technology can be found in some surprising places.* ***Below:*** *Members of the Cosworth team receive the award for UK Manufacturer of the Year 2011.*

ACKNOWLEDGMENTS

The publishers would like to sincerely thank a number of individuals and organisations for their help and contribution to this publication.

Northamptonshire Libraries and Information Service, Northamptonshire Studies

Getty Images - www.gettyimages.co.uk